NAL INSTITUTE OF

OMIC AND SOCIAL RESEARCH

al Papers II

ional
employment Differences
reat Britain

CHESHIRE

erregional
gration Models and
ir Application to
eat Britain

EEDEN

BRIDGE UNIVERSITY PRESS

National Institute

of Economic and Social Research

REGIONAL PAPERS II

REGIONAL UNEMPLOYMENT DIFFERENCES IN GREAT BRITAIN

and

INTERREGIONAL MIGRATION MODELS AND THEIR APPLICATION
TO GREAT BRITAIN

The National Institute of Economic and Social Research is an independent, non-profit-making body, founded in 1938. It has as its aim the promotion of realistic research, particularly in the field of economics. It conducts research by its own research staff and in co-operation with the universities and other academic bodies. The results of the work done under the Institute's auspices are published in several series, and a list of its recent publications will be found at the end of this volume.

Regional Unemployment Differences in Great Britain

by P.C. CHESHIRE

Interregional Migration Models and their Application to Great Britain

by R. WEEDEN

with a foreword by A.J. BROWN

CAMBRIDGE UNIVERSITY PRESS

PUBLISHED BY

THE SYNDICS OF THE CAMBRIDGE UNIVERSITY PRESS

Bentley House, 200 Euston Road, London NW1 2DB

American Branch: 32 East 57th Street, New York, N.Y. 10022

© National Institute of Economic and Social Research 1973

Standard Book Number 0 521 20376 7   )er:

Set in cold type by E.W.C. Wilkins Ltd,
and printed in Great Britain
at the University Printing House, Cambridge

FOREWORD

This is the second volume of a series of working papers arising from research done at the National Institute into problems of regional economic development in the United Kingdom. This work, which began in October 1966, was financed by a grant made originally by the former Department of Economic Affairs, and taken over by the Ministry of Housing, Local Government and Regional Planning. The main conclusions were presented in *The Framework of Regional Economics in the United Kingdom* by A.J. Brown, published by the Cambridge University Press in 1972. A supplementary grant from the Department of the Environment enabled us to edit the two papers presented here.

The first of these papers gives an account of Mr Cheshire's investigations of inter-regional differences in the extent and nature of unemployment. The earlier part of these was quoted briefly in *The Framework of Regional Economics in the United Kingdom*, but space did not make it possible to give there either the detail of the work or the theoretical basis on which the attempt to measure differences between the degrees of imperfection of regional labour markets was based. In this paper account has been taken also of later investigations at the National Institute, completed after the book was written.

Mr Weeden's work on migration models, described in the second paper, began with a survey of the relevant literature, undertaken to help in deciding what kind of analysis of the available British data would be most productive. It was thought that this, as well as the extended version of the British model eventually decided upon (the main results of which were summarised in the book), would be of use to others interested in this field. Both the survey and a full account of the model for Great Britain are accordingly given in this paper.

National Institute of Economic   A.J. BROWN
and Social Research

May 1973

v

CONTENTS

REGIONAL UNEMPLOYMENT DIFFERENCES IN GREAT BRITAIN

LIST OF TABLES

LIST OF CHARTS

INTERREGIONAL MIGRATION MODELS AND THEIR APPLICATION TO GREAT BRITAIN

LIST OF TABLES

LIST OF CHARTS

ACKNOWLEDGEMENTS

ae research team on regional economic development was an unusually co-operative group
ad it was always difficult to distinguish individual from collective effort. But, in particu-
r, we are grateful for Arthur Brown's friendly and informal over-seeing and advice, which
ere quite indispensable. John Bowers also made a major contribution to both these papers
ad we are most grateful for the discussions we had with Ed Webb. Professor Hart and
avid Worswick also contributed much valuable advice and criticism from outside the
amediate group.

ane 1973   P.C.C.
                                                                             R.W.

SYMBOLS USED IN THE TABLES

	Nil
	Not applicable
.a.	Not available

Regional Unemployment Differences in Great Britain

by P.C. CHESHIRE

NTRODUCTION

For as long as there has been an interest in the regional problem in this country, there has been concern over differences in unemployment between regions. Unemployment differences have almost been *the* regional problem; they have certainly been used as a key indicator, indeed, until quite recently perhaps the only indicator, of regional imbalance. The relative position of regions has been remarkably constant for some fifty years. In Great Britain there have been three regions of high unemployment — Scotland, Wales and the North — two intermediate regions — the North West and the South West — and low unemployment elsewhere, in the Midlands and South Eastern England. Positions within groups have changed: before the war unemployment tended to be highest in Wales, whereas more recently Scotland and the North have been worse off; the position of the North West has improved relative to that of the South West since the late 1950s and these intermediate regions have been joined, since 1967, by Yorkshire and Humberside where unemployment has risen. Overall however, the relative unemployment rates have changed very little, with the worst regions having some three times the unemployment level of the best. The differences in regional unemployment both absolutely and relative to the country as a whole are shown in table 1 for the decade 1958—67, and for the first and last nine quarters of the period.

Official concern with varying unemployment rates between different areas of the country predates explicit government recognition of 'regional' problems as such. Even before the first world war, the Royal Commission on the Poor Laws[1] drew attention to the particular problem of unemployment in London as distinct from the prosperous North. For the relative position of the regions was then largely the reverse of what it is today, with the highest unemployment in London and the lowest in Wales, the North and Scotland, but even then the Midlands were comparatively well off.

This is the background against which this paper sets out to examine the nature, and as far as possible the causes, of regional unemployment differences. Data from the middle 1950s to the late 1960s have been used, which has imposed a number of constraints, particularly on the choice of regions. During the period covered, there were three major and a number of minor boundary revisions in the Ministry of Labour regions. This problem was overcome by amalgamation, notably of the various Midland and Yorkshire regions, though occasionally it was possible to analyse them separately; or, for South Eastern England, by extending forward as far as possible the data for the old regions, the East, the South, and London and the South East. Since much of the data does not exist in comparable form for Northern Ireland, it was excluded from the analysis altogether.

---

[1] *Report of the Royal Commission on the Poor Laws and Relief of Distress.* Cd 4499, London, HMSO, 1909.

Table 1.   *Regional unemployment rates and rate relatives,*[a] *December 1958 to December 1967*

Percentage

	North	North West	Cen- tral[b]	London & S.E.	East & South	South West	Wales	Scot- land	Great Britain
Males									
Unemployment rates[c]									
Dec. 1958–Dec. 1967	3·27	2·24	1·32	1·29	1·37	1·87	2·77	3·62	1·88
Dec. 1958–March 1961	2·85	2·23	1·21	1·21	1·40	1·87	2·70	3·81	1·83
Sept. 1965–Dec. 1967	3·56	2·19	1·55	1·53	1·59	2·37	3·43	3·50	2·07
Regional relatives[d]									
Dec. 1958–Dec. 1967	174	119	70	69	73	100	148	193	100
Dec. 1958–March 1961	156	122	66	66	77	102	148	209	100
Sept. 1965–Dec. 1967	172	106	75	74	77	115	166	170	100
Females									
Unemployment rates[c]									
Dec. 1958–Dec. 1967	1·87	1·26	0·75	0·55	0·68	1·08	2·18	2·43	1·05
Dec. 1958–March 1961	2·18	1·56	0·90	0·63	0·86	1·43	2·88	2·77	1·27
Sept. 1965–Dec. 1967	1·45	0·88	0·61	0·43	0·53	1·04	1·95	2·00	0·84
Regional relatives[d]									
Dec. 1958–Dec. 1967	177	119	71	52	65	103	208	231	100
Dec. 1958–March 1961	173	123	71	50	68	113	228	219	100
Sept. 1965–Dec. 1967	172	105	72	51	65	123	231	237	100

SOURCE: *Ministry of Labour Gazette* (various issues)

[a] The data are not seasonally adjusted. These dates and the sub-periods shown have been chosen to produce symmetrical series over the cycle and as far as possible seasonally.

[b] An amalgamation of the various Midland and Yorkshire regions.

[c] Wholly unemployed as a percentage of the total labour force, i.e. employed plus unemployed. Quarterly rates averaged over the periods shown.

[d] Regional unemployment rate as a percentage of the unemployment rate for Great Britain.

The other general qualification is that the analysis concentrated mainly on wholly unemployed adult males. It is unfortunate not to have been able to examine female unemployment so thoroughly, but the official unemployment statistics for the two sexes have different meanings. They relate to the registered unemployed and, whilst it is fairly certain that most unemployed men (and perhaps also single, widowed and divorced women) register as such, it is equally if not more certain that a comparatively large proportion of unemployed married women do not, because married women on becoming unemployed often dissolve into the statistical limbo of the economically inactive. Therefore, whilst it is reasonable to assume that for men officially recorded unemployment is a tolerable approximation to actual unemployment, no such assumption can be made in the case of women. Similar considerations excluded juvenile unemployment from the study.

CHAPTER ONE

REGIONAL UNEMPLOYMENT AS A PROBLEM OF INDUSTRIAL STRUCTURE

It has long been argued that one of the main causes of regional unemployment differences is the location of declining or growing industries in particular regions. The sharp reversal of regional fortunes after the first world war was first explained on these lines by A.L. Bowley,[1] who suggested that the concentrated presence of coalmining and shipbuilding in the North, Wales and Scotland caused their postwar decline just as it had caused their nineteenth century prosperity. What had created employment when world demand was booming, created unemployment when world demand fell.

There are two propositions here. The first is that declining industries show generally high unemployment rates, growing industries low ones. The second is that the unemployment rate is specific to industries rather than to regions, so that a region's unemployment rate can mostly be 'explained' by its industrial composition. As to the former of these, Sir William Beveridge pointed out in 1944 that, on the evidence of changes in employment in individual industries between 1924 and 1937, and the levels of unemployment prevailing in them in those years, 'the connection [between the rate of unemployment in an industry and the growth of effective demand for labour in it] is slight and uncertain'.[2] It will, however, be worth enquiring whether the same conclusion holds for the late 1950s and the 1960s, using regional rather than national statistics. This may be done by simple correlations between the percentage growth of employment by industrial order over a period and the industrial unemployment rate at the end of the period. The results for men and women separately, for Great Britain as a whole and five regions for the period 1959–63, and for Great Britain and eight regions for the period 1960–5, are set out in table 2.

Table 2 shows some negative relationships, within particular regions, between employment growth in an industry and its unemployment rate. In only three out of the 30 cases was the association positive, and none of these coefficients was remotely significant on a t test (one was in fact zero after rounding). Of the 27 negative coefficients, 11 were significant. There was therefore some tendency for slow or negative industrial growth to be associated with an industrial unemployment rate higher than average, and vice versa. It was only a very slight tendency however, the highest R^2 being 0·51. There were more significant correlations for females than for males (nine compared with two), probably because the two most consistently 'aberrant' industries, mining and quarrying, and construction, employ mainly males. This point is discussed in more detail below.

---

[1] A.L. Bowley, *Some Economic Consequences of the Great War*, London, Butterworth, 1930.
Sir William Beveridge also made the point in 'An analysis of unemployment' (part 1), *Economica*, vol. 3, November 1936, pp. 357–86.

[2] W.H. Beveridge, *Full Employment in a Free Society*, London, Allen and Unwin, 1944, p. 52.

Table 2. *Correlations of employment growth and unemployment rates by industrial order*

	Males			Females		
	R	R²	t	R	R²	t
Growth 1959–63 and unemployment 1963						
North	−0·21	0·04	−1·05	−0·40*	0·16*	−2·28
North West	−0·27	0·07	−1·39	−0·44*	0·19*	−2·61
South West	−0·29	0·08	−1·51	−0·28	0·07	−1·44
Wales	−0·34	0·12	−1·85	−0·07	—	−0·35
Scotland	−0·40*	0·16*	−2·28	−0·48*	0·23*	−2·99
Great Britain	−0·14	0·02	−0·72	−0·72*	0·51*	−7·05
Growth 1960–5 and unemployment 1965						
North	—	—	—	−0·31	0·10	−1·69
North West	−0·15	0·02	−0·77	−0·38*	0·14*	−2·16
Central	−0·08	0·01	−0·41	−0·13	0·02	−0·64
London and South East	−0·12	0·01	−0·60	−0·71*	0·50*	−6·92
East and South	+0·03	—	+0·14	+0·04	—	+0·20
South West	−0·21	0·05	−1·10	−0·36	0·13	−1·99
Wales	−0·43*	0·18*	−2·56	−0·50*	0·25*	−3·30
Scotland	−0·14	0·02	−0·68	−0·46*	0·21*	2·89
Great Britain	−0·22	0·05	−1·16	−0·66*	0·43*	−5·64

SOURCES: NIESR estimates based on *Ministry of Labour Gazette* and tabulations supplied by the Department of Employment and Productivity.

Note: An asterisk (∗) indicates significance at the 5 per cent level.

If the industrial growth rates and unemployment rates are plotted out, various points of interest emerge. There were some 'conforming' industries, which consistently displayed large negative growth and high unemployment rates in all regions and for both sexes. Shipbuilding and marine engineering did so in all regions except one: in the combined Central region, male employment in this industry did not change between 1960 and 1965 and female employment increased by 50 per cent, yet in 1965 it had a higher unemployment rate for males than any other industry in the region and the second highest female unemployment rate. Probably this results from combining the very small shipbuilding industry in the Midlands, concerned mostly with small boat manufacture, with a larger section in Yorkshire (and Humberside) engaged in the more traditional work of the industry. Small boat building and shipbuilding are for many purposes entirely separate, and to some extent it is an accident of the Standard Industrial Classification that they are grouped together.

There were other 'conforming' industries which showed uniformly high growth and low unemployment, such as professional and scientific services, and insurance, banking and finance. There were also a number of 'aberrant' industries, such as construction and miscellaneous services, which combined high growth with a high unemployment rate in nearly all regions for both men and women. In contrast mining and quarrying, and vehicle manufacture tended to have negative or low rates of growth with low unemployment. The results for miscellaneous services and construction might illustrate another shortcoming of the statistics, in that the unemployed are classified according to the last industry in which they worked, so that industries which have a large proportion of short-term and casual employees are credited with unemployed who in fact have more past experience elsewhere.

Over the whole range of industrial orders, then, there was some tendency for slow or negative growth to be associated with high unemployment and for fast growth to be associated with low unemployment. This tendency was not very strong and was weaker for men than for women. Our more recent and detailed data confirm Beveridge's findings.

The second proposition mentioned above was that a region's general unemployment rate depends on its structure. Total unemployment in a region can be recalculated on different hypotheses: what it would have been if the region had had the national industrial structure but its own rate of unemployment in each industry,[1] and what it would have been if it had had its own industrial structure but the national unemployment rate in each of its industries.[2] The difference between the former and the actual unemployment rate will be a measure of the direct effect of the region's industrial structure on its overall unemployment. The difference between the latter and the actual unemployment rate will measure how much of the region's unemployment was due to higher or lower unemployment rates in its individual industries than in those industries in the country as a whole.

The results of these standardisations in different regions at two dates are set out in table 3 for men and for women separately. The data on which they are based suffer (apart from other shortcomings, already mentioned) from the fact that there are some unemployed not classified by industry; in different regions the proportion varied from 6 to 12 per cent for men and from 13 to 21 per cent for women. There is, however, no tendency for these proportions to be related to regional unemployment rates, and, that being so, it does not seem likely that their existence will invalidate the use of the regional figures, excluding the unclassified, for comparison with the results of standardisation.

The standardisations for men in 1963 show that in no region did the industrial structure 'explain' an unemployment rate difference from the national average of more than 0·28 per cent. Both Scotland and Wales, which had overall unemployment rates well above that of the nation, were affected by this amount, but whereas in Wales the industrial structure marginally reduced unemployment, in Scotland it marginally raised it. The North was the only other region where the effect of industrial structure was more than 0·10 per cent; like Scotland, it had an 'unfavourable' structure which apparently increased unemployment. In all other regions the direct effects of industrial structure were 0·09 per cent or less, and after rounding their significance must be doubtful. Certainly industrial structure provides no direct general explanation of the divergences between regional and national unemployment rates: it was apparently favourable in two of the four regions with higher than national unemployment rates, and unfavourable in two of the six regions with lower than national unemployment rates.

In contrast, there was a very marked tendency for unemployment rates in all industries in a region to diverge similarly from the national industrial rates. This part of the regional difference had in all cases the same sign as the total difference, and was of similar magnitude. If regions all had national unemployment rates in their industries, regional unemployment differences would nearly disappear. The standard deviation of male unemployment rates in 1963 standardised for industrial unemployment rates $(U_{in} \cdot P_{ir})$ was 0·126, compared with 1·226 for actual regional unemployment rates and 1·154 for the rates standardised for industrial structure, $(U_{ir} \cdot P_{in})$.

---

[1] $\Sigma_i U_{ir} \cdot P_{in}$, where U is the unemployment rate, P the proportion of the labour force, i refers to an industry, r to a region and n to the national level.

[2] $\Sigma_i U_{in} \cdot P_{ir}$.

Table 3. *Industrial structure and industrial unemployment rates as explanations of regional unemployment differences*

Percentage

	North	Yorks. & Lincs.[a]	North West	Mid-lands	London & S.E.	East & South	South West	Wales	Scotland
Males, June 1963									
Actual unemployment rates[b]	4·33	1·64	2·83	1·45	1·37	1·31	1·70	2·70	4·3
Differences from national rate[c]	+2·20	−0·49	+0·70	−0·68	−0·76	−0·82	−0·43	+0·57	+2·2
Rates standardised for:									
Industrial structure	4·21	1·73	2·88	1·51	1·36	1·34	1·64	2·98	4·0
Industrial unemployment rates	2·34	2·09	2·11	1·98	2·13	2·16	2·25	2·10	2·3
Differences explained by:									
Industrial structure	+0·12	−0·09	−0·05	−0·06	+0·01	−0·03	+0·06	−0·28	+0·2
Industrial unemployment rates	+1·99	−0·45	+0·72	−0·53	−0·76	−0·85	−0·55	+0·60	+1·9
Residual	+0·09	+0·05	+0·03	−0·09	−0·01	+0·06	+0·06	+0·25	−0·0
Males, June 1965									
Actual unemployment rates[b]	2·23	1·00	1·58	0·69	0·88	0·86	1·42	2·07	2·5
Differences from national rate[d]	+0·96	−0·27	+0·31	−0·58	−0·39	−0·41	+0·15	+0·80	+1·2
Rates standardised for:									
Industrial structure	2·25	1·08	1·61	0·76	0·85	0·89	1·37	2·32	2·4
Industrial unemployment rates	1·32	1·21	1·23	1·14	1·31	1·27	1·34	1·23	1·3
Differences explained by:									
Industrial structure	−0·02	−0·08	−0·03	−0·07	+0·03	−0·03	+0·05	−0·25	+0·1
Industrial unemployment rates	+0·91	−0·21	+0·35	−0·45	−0·43	−0·41	+0·08	+0·84	+1·1
Residual	+0·07	+0·02	−0·01	−0·06	+0·01	+0·03	+0·02	+0·21	−0·0
Females, June 1963									
Actual unemployment rates[b]	2·38	0·90	1·70	0·81	0·60	0·69	0·85	2·03	2·6
Differences from national rate[e]	+1·20	−0·28	+0·52	−0·37	−0·58	−0·49	−0·33	+0·85	+1·5
Rates standardised for:									
Industrial structure	2·44	0·90	1·65	0·79	0·61	0·70	0·86	2·15	2·9
Industrial unemployment rates	1·16	1·24	1·25	1·23	1·14	1·14	1·14	1·13	1·1
Differences explained by:									
Industrial structure	−0·06	—	+0·05	+0·02	−0·01	−0·01	−0·01	−0·12	−0·2
Industrial unemployment rates	+1·22	−0·34	+0·45	−0·42	−0·54	−0·45	−0·29	+0·90	+1·5
Residual	+0·04	+0·06	+0·02	+0·03	−0·03	−0·03	−0·03	+0·07	+0·1
Females, June 1965									
Actual employment rates[b]	1·14	0·46	0·77	0·34	0·32	0·37	0·53	1·33	1·5
Differences from national rate[f]	+0·53	−0·15	+0·16	−0·27	−0·29	−0·24	−0·08	+0·72	+0·9
Rates standardised for:									
Industrial structure	1·18	0·48	0·75	0·34	0·32	0·37	0·52	1·45	1·6
Industrial unemployment rates	0·61	0·62	0·62	0·62	0·61	0·60	0·61	0·58	0·6
Differences explained by:									
Industrial structure	−0·04	−0·02	+0·02	—	—	—	+0·01	−0·12	−0·0
Industrial unemployment rates	+0·53	−0·16	+0·15	−0·28	−0·29	−0·23	−0·08	+0·75	+0·9
Residual	+0·04	+0·03	−0·01	+0·01	—	−0·01	−0·01	+0·09	+0·0

SOURCE: as table 2.

[a] Yorks. and Humberside in 1965.

[b] Excluding unemployed not classified by industry.

[c] National rate 2·13 per cent, excluding unemployed not classified by industry.

[d] National rate 1·27 per cent, excluding unemployed not classified by industry.

[e] National rate 1·18 per cent, excluding unemployed not classified by industry.

[f] National rate 0·61 per cent, excluding unemployed not classified by industry.

As for the residual deviation of regional from national unemployment not explained by either of these standardisations, only in Wales did it appear considerable; probably because the industries concentrated there showed lower unemployment than in the country at large, and industries under-represented there greater unemployment. Coalmining and metal manufacture are both concentrated in Wales but had a lower unemployment rate here than nationally, and engineering, shipbuilding, vehicles and distribution were all under-represented in Wales but had higher than national unemployment rates there. This tendency was, however, not statistically significant.[1]

The general pattern of the other results was very similar to that for men in June 1963. All suggest, at least superficially, that the industrial structure of a region was virtually irrelevant in determining its unemployment rate, for both men and women, and at times of high or of low unemployment. By June 1965 the unemployment rate for men in Great Britain had fallen to 1·27 per cent compared with 2·13 per cent in June 1963. Unemployment had, however, increased substantially in relative terms in Wales and the South West, but it had fallen relatively in the North West, the Midlands and the North. In both regions where unemployment had risen relatively the effect of industrial structure was unchanged, but the effect of industrial unemployment rates (the 'regional' effect) increased markedly in Wales (from +0·60 to +0·84) and in the South West (from −0·55 to −0·08). In the regions where unemployment fell relatively, the regional effect was substantially reduced where unemployment was above average (from +0·72 to +0·35 in the North West and from +1·99 to +0·91 in the North) and became only slightly less favourable in the Midlands. Only in the North did the effect of industrial structure alter appreciably, from +0·12 in 1963 to −0·02 in 1965, but this latter figure is so small that its significance is doubtful. Wales continued to be the only region with a residual exceeding ·10. The analysis of female unemployment shows little difference between 1963 and 1965.

To check whether the results were affected by the degree of industrial aggregation some similar standardisations were done, for men only, with industries classified by minimum list heading. The published breakdown of unemployment by region and industry made it possible to do this using 53 industries on figures for June 1963 for London and the South East, the North and Scotland. The results for these three regions make it sufficiently clear that the level of industrial disaggregation does not greatly affect the general result of the calculation: industrial structure continued to have little apparent effect on a region's unemployment rate. The only change that was even slightly significant was in London and the South East, where the greater disaggregation suggested that the effect of industrial structure, instead of being neutral, was very marginally to reduce unemployment.

A standardisation at industrial order level was also done for a more recent date, March 1967, although a combination of regional boundary changes and other data problems severely limited the number of regions for which it was possible to calculate comparable rates. Unemployment nationally was then comparatively high, with low demand aggravated by seasonal factors, the rate for men being 2·66 per cent. Unemployment in the South West, which is particularly sensitive seasonally, was relatively and absolutely higher than in 1963, indeed the rate was above that for Great Britain as a whole. Unemployment in Scotland was relatively and absolutely lower than in 1963. Despite these

[1] An across-industry correlation for Wales of $P_{ir} - P_{in}$ against $U_{ir} - U_{in}$ yielded an R of −0·34 ($R^2 = 0·12$): the associated value of t was 1·90, which is not significant with 23 degrees of freedom.

differences, the effect of industrial structure as measured by the standardisations was almost the same – more or less neutral in the South West, but somewhat unfavourable in Scotland. The residual for Scotland was rather larger than at either of the two previous dates, and its sign indicated that industries concentrated in Scotland were doing rather worse than elsewhere and industries under-represented were doing rather better. Nevertheless, differences between regional and national unemployment continued to be 'explained' almost exclusively by interregional differences in unemployment rates within industries.

One other standardisation was tried, using unweighted means of regional figures instead of national average figures of structure and unemployment rates, which are very dependent on the values for South East England and the Midlands. This is in some ways nearer to the analysis of variance considered below which is concerned with deviations of regional figures from unweighted means rather than from national means. Again the results were almost indistinguishable in essentials from those in table 3. The mean regional unemployment rate was naturally higher than the national average rate (for men, 2·43 per cent in June 1963) because of the changed regional weights. The apparent differences in low-unemployment regions were therefore increased and those in high-unemployment regions decreased. The relative importance of the structural and regional effects and the residuals, however, remained virtually unchanged.

This analysis appears to show that industrial structure was almost entirely irrelevant to regional unemployment differences, anyhow for the periods studied, which is to say the least, an unexpected result. That conclusion, however, would not be justified. Since labour can transfer between industries, unemployment is unlikely to be industrially specific at least in the medium term. Decline in any industry raises unemployment in other industries in an area. Regions where high-unemployment industries are concentrated may therefore tend to have high unemployment in all industries, and vice versa for regions with mainly low-unemployment industries.

The significance of the effects of industry and region was next tested by an unweighted analysis of variance for two dates, June 1963 and June 1965, and for men and women separately. Here it was also possible to test for interaction, to see whether the classifications of unemployment rates by region and industry are really independent, or whether unemployment in high-unemployment industries tends to be systematically higher than expected in high-unemployment regions and vice versa. The results are set out in table 4.

In all cases the variance between regions was much greater than between industries, although perhaps not so much as might have been expected from the standardisations. For men the ratio was about two to one; for women about nine to one. The difference between men and women in the importance of industrial structure was not nearly so marked in the standardisations. Indeed, in the sums of squares where there was no allowance for the greater number of industries than of regions, industry appeared more important than region for men, although not for women. In all, the classifications by region and industry accounted for between 66·0 per cent and 76·4 per cent of the total sum of squares, leaving an unexplained residual varying from 23·6 to 34·0 per cent. In all cases both region and industry were significant on an F test at 0·1 per cent.

Testing for interaction, however, gave a highly significant positive result in all cases. For men, the value of F for the interaction component was much higher than for either of the other variables; for women, F for the regional component was rather higher than

	Sum of squares		Degrees of freedom	Variance	Value of F
	Total	Percentage			
Aales 1963					
Region	203·445	28·4	8	25·431*	27·705
Industry	343·749	48·0	23	14·946*	16·282
Residual	168·895	23·6	184	0·918	
Total	716·089	100·0			
Interaction	*45·869*	*6·4*	*1*	*45·869**	*68·231*
Aales 1965					
Region	75·081	29·1	8	9·385*	19·717
Industry	95·050	36·9	23	4·133*	8·682
Residual	87·592	34·0	184	0·476	
Total	257·723	100·0			
Interaction	*12·276*	*4·8*	*1*	*12·276**	*29·827*
Females 1963					
Region	210·992	51·7	8	26·374*	47·444
Industry	94·569	23·2	23	4·112*	7·397
Residual	102·282	25·1	184	0·556	
Total	407·843	100·0			
Interaction	*8·866*	*2·2*	*1*	*8·866**	*17·368*
Females 1965					
Region	76·876	60·2	8	9·610*	57·165
Industry	19·824	15·5	23	0·862*	5·127
Residual	30·928	24·2	184	0·168	
Total	127·628	100·0	*1*	*2·798**	*18·205*
Interaction	*2·798*	*2·2*			

SOURCES: as table 2.

Note: An asterisk (*) indicates significance at the 0·1 per cent level.

for interaction, but the latter was still highly significant. This degree of interaction suggests that no firm conclusions can be drawn from this analysis about the independent effects of region and industry on the unemployment rate observed in an industry in a particular region. Unemployment in a high-unemployment industry in a high-unemployment region tends to be higher than can be accounted for simply by the general disadvantage of the industry throughout the country and the disadvantage of other industries in the region. In other words, high unemployment tends to be 'localised' in particular industries in particular regions; and the same is true of low unemployment.

This implies not only that labour is imperfectly mobile both within industries and within regions, but also that a given industry has in many cases a different character in different regions. The declining industry with high unemployment in a high-unemployment region might differ from the industry classified in the same order elsewhere in the country. Shipbuilding has already been cited as a possible example of this; another might be the vehicle industry, which consists mainly of motor-car manufacture in one region and the construction of railway locomotives in another. The interaction observed could therefore result from too high a degree of industrial aggregation, but to disaggregate, even if the data allowed it, would not necessarily provide an answer. What would be the proper egree of disaggregation? To make all classifications entirely homogeneous might require disaggregation down to establishment level. Each 'industry' would then appear in only one region, and all forms of analysis that depend on distinguishing a 'regional' effect wou become impossible.

CHAPTER TWO

A CLASSIFICATION OF UNEMPLOYMENT

Ever since the publication of Keynes's *General Theory* in 1936,[1] unemployment has been viewed mainly as the result of deficiency of effective demand. Before that time however, classifications of unemployment had been attempted which distinguished some categories for which demand-deficiency cannot be held responsible. Beveridge, in his first study of unemployment published in 1909, suggested that seasonal and cyclical fluctuations in demand for labour were important causes of unemployment,[2] but other categories in the pre-Keynesian era were 'frictional' and 'structural' unemployment, which were both regarded by Beveridge in his 1944 report as consequences of labour-market imperfections.[3] Frictional unemployment was defined as 'unemployment caused by the individuals who make up the labour supply not being completely interchangeable and mobile units, so that though there is an unsatisfied demand for labour, the unemployed workers are not of the right sort or in the right place to meet that demand'. Structural unemployment was 'that arising in particular industries or localities through a change of demand so great that it may be regarded as affecting the main economic structures of a country... Structural unemployment may or may not be a form of frictional unemployment'. The remainder of this paper attempts to identify different types of unemployment in something like this way, and to assess their causes and importance. This may help towards providing a more substantial base for policies designed to relieve regional unemployment differences. The most effective remedy for these differences is bound to depend on their cause and, if Keynesian demand-deficiency should not be the sole, or even the most important reason, Keynesian remedies alone cannot be expected to eliminate the problem.

In recent writing a number of somewhat similar classifications of unemployment have been revived. In the United States, attention has been focused on the persistently high level of unemployment which, even in 1964 after four years of continuous expansion, was still 5·2 per cent, very much higher than in what was claimed to be a comparable period in the early 1950s. The discussion of the causes of this phenomenon polarised into 'structuralist' and 'demand-deficiency' theories. Very simply, the former argued that a change had taken place in the skill structure of employment to which the labour force had been unable to adapt, resulting in a growing pool of unemployed, unable to find jobs not because there were none available, but because their skills (or possibly their location) were unsuitable for the vacancies.[4] The demand-deficiency theory was simply that the economy of the United States had been running at an insufficiently high level of aggregate

---

[1] J.M. Keynes, *General Theory of Employment, Interest and Money,* London, Macmillan, 1936.

[2] W.H. Beveridge, *Unemployment: a problem of industry,* London, Longmans Green, 1909.

[3] Beveridge, *Full Employment in a Free Society.*

[4] See, for example, G. Myrdal, *Challenge to Affluence,* London, Gollancz, 1963.

11

demand.[1] This discussion is used as a background to the investigation of regional unemployment differences in this paper, although here the concern is with spatial rather than temporal unemployment differences.

R.G. Lipsey attempted to combine the structuralist and demand-deficiency theories by linking structural unemployment to the 'Phillips' relationship between the unemployment rate and the rate of change of wages.[2] He suggested that, assuming such a relationship, structural unemployment should be defined as that which remained at the maximum acceptable rate of increase of prices.[3] Unemployment could only be reduced below this level by moving the curve downwards and to the left. In the context of the American debate, such a definition would require the curve to have moved away from the origin over time. In the context of this paper, if differences in structural unemployment were a contributory factor in regional unemployment differences, Lipsey's definition would require the curves for each region (or more precisely the sectors of the curves on which regions were operating) to lie at different distances from the origin.

To come, however, to the classification that it is intended to use here; it depends upon the fact that, in Great Britain, statistics of unfilled vacancies are available, as well as statistics of numbers unemployed. In fact, the recording of vacancies may be far from complete, and the degree of incompleteness probably varies with the state of the labour market. Indeed, British unemployment statistics, also, are incomplete as a record of involuntary worklessness. It is easiest to start, however, by supposing that we have complete statistics of both unfilled vacancies and unemployment. If this is assumed, the following definitions can, in principle, be applied:

(a) Frictional unemployment consists of all those unemployed persons for whom there appear to be vacancies in the categories in which they are registered. The frictionally unemployed in any industry[4] are thus the number unemployed or the number of vacancies, whichever is smaller, and the total for the region is the sum of these numbers across all industries.

(b) Structural unemployment consists of those for whom there are no vacancies in their own categories in the region, but for whom there would be vacancies if they could change their category. The number of them, so defined, is the total of excesses of vacancies over unemployment in all industries where there is such an excess, or of unemployment over vacancies (where there is such an excess), whichever of the two is smaller.

(c) Demand-deficiency unemployment is the number of unemployed for whom there are no vacancies in the region even if they change their industries. It is the excess of total unemployment over total unfilled vacancies, if there is such an excess. If not, then demand-deficiency unemployment is zero.

These three definitions have the merit that the classes of unemployment they represent

---

[1] See R.M. Solow 'The nature and sources of unemployment in the United States' in *Wicksell Lectures 1964*, Stockholm, Almquist and Wicksell, 1964.

[2] R.G. Lipsey, 'Structural and deficient demand unemployment reconsidered' in Arthur M. Ross (ed.), *Employment and the Labor Market*, Berkeley (Cal.), University of California Press, 1965.

[3] The rate of increase of prices being assumed to be a function of the rate of increase of wages.

[4] Industry is only one possible category; skill or occupation might be more appropriate in some cases. However, the choice is limited in practice by the form of data available.

ld up to total unemployment. Take for instance a two-industry economy[1] with unemployment U_1 and U_2, vacancies V_1 and V_2 in its two industries. If $V_1 > U_1$, $V_2 < U_2$, then frictional unemployment is $U_1 + V_2$. Structural unemployment is $V_1 - U_1$ or $U_2 - V_2$ whichever is smaller. Demand-deficiency unemployment is $U_1 + U_2 - V_1 - V_2$, or $(U_2 - V_2) - (V_1 - U_1)$. For this to be positive, $U_2 - V_2$ must be greater than $V_1 - U_1$, and the latter is therefore the expression that represents structural unemployment. This being so, it is readily shown that the three kinds of unemployment add up to $U_1 + U_2$, which is total unemployment in the economy. If there is excess demand in the economy — that is an excess of total vacancies over total unemployment, implying a negative amount of demand-deficiency and zero demand-deficiency unemployment — then structural and frictional unemployment as defined above add up to $U_1 + U_2$, the actual unemployment total.

There are, however, some features about this set of definitions that seem unsatisfactory at first sight. The first is that how much unemployment is classified as frictional may depend greatly on the size of the area for which the calculation is done. A large area will tend to show a lot of unemployment as frictional, simply because unemployed in one part of it are not readily available for jobs in their industry that exist a hundred miles away. If the calculation is done for single labour exchange areas, such unemployment will tend to appear as structural because there are a lot of the unemployed for whom there are jobs in their own industries in other areas, but who, in relation to the opportunities in their own exchange areas, have the wrong skills. It would be interesting, if one had the data, to divide the frictionally unemployed for the whole region into those for whom there are vacancies in their own industries in their own areas and those for whom such vacancies exist elsewhere in the region. This last section of unemployment might be called 'locational'.

The second feature of the classification that warrants a critical inspection is the sensitivity of the relations between the three classes distinguished to the general level of unemployment. This is in the nature of the definitions. If pressure of demand is so low that there are no unfilled vacancies, all unemployment will be classed as due to demand-deficiency — there are no vacant employment opportunities for the unemployed either in their own industries or in any others for which they might retrain. But as effective demand is increased and demand-deficiency unemployment shrinks, unfilled vacancies appear, and with them an equal amount of (initially) frictional unemployment, which offsets part of the reduction in the demand-deficiency category. As soon as vacancies in any industry exceed unemployment in it, part of the growth of frictional unemployment turns into a growth of structural unemployment instead. At some point there ceases to be an aggregate deficiency of demand, and all unemployment is then either frictional or structural. The latter, however, would cease to exist if the point were reached where vacancies exceeded unemployment in every industry; the remaining unemployment (presumably small) would then all be classed as frictional.

The practical use of this kind of classification, therefore (in so far as the statistical sources enable it to be applied), does not lie in its providing directly a theoretical prescription for getting unemployment down to zero (or to some minimum level of frictional unemployment). A classification into, say, 1 per cent frictional unemployment, 2 per cent

[1] The conclusions in fact hold for an economy of any number of industries since these can always be grouped into two classes — those in which $V > U$, and those in which $U > V$ — and the argument can then proceed as above.

structural, and 3 per cent demand-deficiency, does not mean that increasing demand by 3 per cent and retraining 2 per cent of employees would leave only 1 per cent frictional unemployment. The increase in demand would alter structural and frictional unemployment: some of it would pile up vacancies for which potential applicants existed but were not yet recruited (perhaps because they lived a long way off), and some of it would increase the number of vacancies for which there were insufficient candidates in the required trades, though others might be made available by retraining. What the analysis does indicate is, very roughly, whether extra demand, or retraining, or improved information and geographical mobility of labour, or some combination of these, is likely to be the thing most required to produce *some* reduction of unemployment. More especially, it shows how regions, at a given point of time, differ in this respect.

Nevertheless, there is more to be said about the unemployment prevailing in a region than that, at a given date, it was divided between the kinds described in a certain way. One could, for instance, perform the classification for different points of time when the levels of total unemployment were different, and try to draw up schedules of amount of frictional, structural and demand-deficiency unemployment at these different levels of total unemployment. There are, however, theoretical considerations which suggest that it may be more profitable to concentrate, as a basis for comparison between regions, on estimating the levels of unemployment in them which are associated with zero demand-deficiency unemployment — that is to say, where total unemployment equals total vacancies.

If complete records of unemployment and unfilled vacancies in a region were plotted against each other over a period of time during which demand for labour varied, one would expect the resulting curve to slope downwards, since increased demand would cause unemployment to fall and unfilled vacancies to rise. One might also expect that, at low levels of unemployment, extra demand for labour would result in the creation of relatively many unfilled vacancies, with a relatively small reduction in the numbers unemployed, because the remaining unemployed became increasingly hard to draw into jobs. (If there were no unemployed, an increase in demand would obviously increase vacancies without reducing unemployment at all.) On the other hand, at high levels of unemployment, decreased demand would tend to throw extra people out of work without a corresponding elimination of unfilled vacancies. If demand was so slack that there were no vacancies, a further slackening, though it would raise unemployment, would clearly not make any difference to the vacancy figures. In other words, unemployment and vacancies necessarily have limiting values of zero, when demand is very low and very high respectively. One might thus expect the functional relation between unemployment and vacancies to be convex to the origin.

If the curve AB in chart 1 is such a relationship between unemployment and vacancies (it is drawn for clarity as extending to the axes, although in real life neither vacancies nor unemployment actually become zero), then a line drawn through the origin at 45° to both axes will cut the curve at C, where unemployment and vacancies are equal to each other and to OD. The graph of demand-deficiency unemployment will be the curve EDF, where OE = OA (at the level of vacancies when unemployment vanishes), and F, the point where the curve meets the 45° line, is vertically above B, the point at which vacancies vanish. The negative part of it, DE, however, signifies excess total demand for labour, and if one is interested only in unemployment it has no useful meaning.

The line DF (the positive part of demand-deficiency unemployment plotted against

Chart 1.   *The unemployment-vacancy relation and demand-deficiency unemployment*

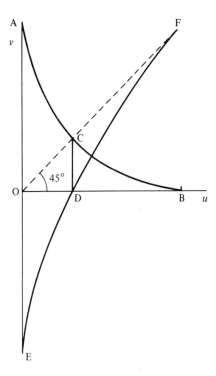

Chart 2.   *The components of unemployment (first definitions)*

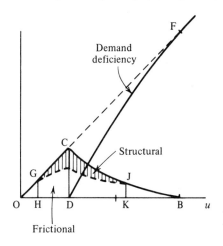

otal unemployment) may, however, be transferred to a new diagram, chart 2, where total
ınemployment is (as before) measured horizontally, but the components of unemploy-
nent, rather than total vacancies, are measured vertically. Non-demand-deficiency unem-
ıloyment (the total of frictional and structural) is very easily drawn in by measuring up
rom the baseline distances equal to the vertical gap between demand-deficiency unem-
ıloyment, DF, and total unemployment as represented by the 45° line. It clearly shows a

15

sharp peak C at (and equal in height to) the unemployment level where demand-deficiency is zero. This peak level of non-demand-deficiency unemployment would seem to be a useful measure of the different degrees to which regions are subject to frictional and structural unemployment (combined); it can in principle be estimated from the relation between unemployment and vacancies calculated from time-series.

It is perhaps worth drawing in on chart 2 the probable graph of frictional unemployment at different hypothetical levels of total unemployment. At very low levels of unemployment, vacancies are likely to exceed unemployment in every industry or occupation and the unemployment is all frictional. At some point (say H), unemployment passes vacancies in some industry or occupation and structural unemployment appears, represented by the distance by which the frictional unemployment graph falls below OC. At a still higher level of total unemployment, K, unemployment passes vacancies in the last industry or occupation where this has not happened already, and all unemployment is once again frictional — the graph joins CB again at J. It is likely, though not certain, that structural unemployment (the vertical gap between frictional and frictional-plus-structural) will, like that sub-total, show a maximum at D, the level of total unemployment corresponding to zero demand-deficiency.

This suggests a modification of the above classification, which should increase its practical usefulness. For levels of unemployment up to that where it equals the number of vacancies, the division between frictional and structural remains exactly as before. Above this point, however, amounts of frictional and structural unemployment are regarded as constant (unchanging as total unemployment rises) and the remainder of unemployment is attributed to demand-deficiency. On these definitions demand-deficiency unemployment is the excess of total unemployment over the level at which that total *would* equal the number of vacancies, instead of being its excess over the number of vacancies actually prevailing at the time. It is thus the minimum amount of unemployment that has to be eliminated in order that only structural and frictional should be left. Structural and frictional unemployment together are either the level of total unemployment at which that total would equal the number of vacancies, or the actual unemployment total whichever is the smaller. Structural and frictional unemployment separately may be defined (as already mentioned) exactly as before for levels of total unemployment equal to or lower than the level of vacancies, but for higher levels they are the amounts that would prevail (according to the original definitions) if total unemployment were at such a level as to be equal to total vacancies. The relation between the new definitions may be clarified by chart 3.

These definitions give (as the original ones do not) the amounts of the three kinds of unemployment that would have to be eliminated in the course of passing from the situation under consideration to one of zero unemployment, assuming that the kinds of extra demand for labour which are created in this process are as well (or as badly) related to the kinds of labour available as has been the case in that region in the past. They could, in principle, be estimated from the complete statistics of unemployment (U) and vacancies (V) in each industrial or occupational group (whichever of the two is considered more relevant) in the region in question at a time when its total unemployment and total unfilled vacancies were equal. The sum of frictional and structural unemployment (what may be called 'non-demand-deficiency' unemployment) would, of course, be immediately calculable, since it is the level of unemployment at which it is equal to vacancies, and this sum expressed as a percentage of the labour force, is probably the best indicator of the imper-

16

Chart 3. *The components of unemployment (revised definitions)*

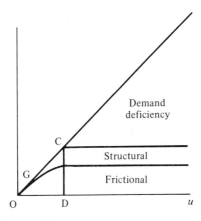

In the chart: Demand deficiency; Structural; Frictional; points C, G, O, D; axis labelled u.

ection of the regional labour market.

In practice, however, there are two obstacles to discovering the level of non-demand-deficiency unemployment in this simple way. The first is that the statistics for some regions cover a range of values within which the point $U = V$ does not lie. If that were all, however, one could hope to overcome it by extrapolation, provided always that the empirical relation between U and V is close enough, and that it has not changed over the period to which the data relate.

The second obstacle is the imperfection of the statistics. As was noted earlier the totals for unfilled vacancies are subject to an unknown degree of under-recording; unemployment statistics for men are also incomplete, though probably less so than for women. The recording ratios of both series have been examined by previous writers. In the past most concern was expressed about the vacancy data, but more recently the propensity to register as unemployed has given rise to discussion.[1] Dow and Dicks-Mireaux concluded that the 'statement' ratio for vacancies was in fact about unity.[2] They based their view, first, on the similarity of the amplitude of seasonal (or cyclical) fluctuations of vacancies to that of unemployment fluctuations; in the light of more recent criticisms of the unemployment series one might take this simply as indicating that the recording ratios for the two series were similar. Their view was based, secondly, on the internal Ministry of Labour analysis of the changes in vacancy levels which occurred when compulsory use of the exchanges was first removed in 1950, then restored in 1952, and finally abandoned in 1956. This analysis showed that, although there was a marked change in the size of the flow of placings taking place through the exchanges, there was a negligible effect on the stock of unfilled vacancies, a finding which they explained in terms of the presumed shape of the vacancy duration curve. Their conclusion was that it was 'certainly possible to form a fairly good though imperfect idea of the extent of statement error; and in our opinion the positioning of the full employment, or zero excess demand point [defined basically as in

[1] See, for example, G. Standing, 'The distribution of concealed unemployment in Great Britain', and N. Bosanquet and G. Standing, 'Government and unemployment, 1966–70: a study of policy and evidence', *British Journal of Industrial Relations,* vol. 10, no. 2, 1972, and the reply, J.K. Bowers, 'Unemployment statistics, 1966–70; a note', *British Journal of Industrial Relations,* vol.11, no.2, 1973.

[2] J.C.R. Dow and L.A. Dicks-Mireaux, 'The excess demand for labour: a study of conditions in Great Britain, 1946–56', *Oxford Economic Papers,* vol. 10, February 1958, pp. 1–33.

this paper] is probably not in error by more than about ±0·25 per cent.' They, in comme with others, such as A.P. Thirlwall[1] and the present writer, found vacancies a satisfactor series with which to work at least as an indicator, though there must remain a real doubt as to the exact 'statement' or recording ratio. The exact relationship between the point where $U = V$ estimated from recorded statistics and the equality of *true* unemployment and vacancies is, therefore, uncertain, and may change over time. If the recording ratio is lower for vacancies than for unemployment, as it might be for men, then the relevant radial should be inclined at less than 45° to the unemployment axis. It could for instance be that the true values of unemployment and vacancies are equal where recorded unemployment is twice the level of recorded vacancies.

Given these two problems it seems prudent in what follows to consider ratios of recorded vacancies to recorded unemployment which are closer to the general run of regional experience than simply that point where recorded unemployment is equal to vacancies, and to see whether the relative incidence of non-demand-deficiency unemploy ment deduced from regional data is greatly altered.

The percentage rate of non-demand-deficiency unemployment may be presented as a measure of the inefficiency of a regional labour market. It is, however, perhaps worth mentioning an alternative indicator that can be derived from the relation between unemployment and unfilled vacancies. This is the rate of change of the former with the latter (dU/dV), measured at some conventional ratio of U to V – most simply, at the point where they are equal. Presumably a labour market may be said to be 'efficient' in a certai sense if an increase in labour demand produces a relatively small increase in the number c unfilled vacancies; that is to say, if, as demand changes, dU/dV is large. This criterion of efficiency, however, is clearly not independent of (although it is not uniquely related to) the level of non-demand-deficiency unemployment, estimated as the level at which $U = V$ on the assumption that the statistics of the two variables are both complete, or at any rat incomplete to similar extents. The value at which $U = V$, calculated from a linear relation between the two of the form $U = a + bV$, is $a/(1 - b)$. As between a number of regions with different linear relations of U to V, the values at which $U = V$ will stand in inverse order to the numerical values of the various coefficients, b or dU/dV, so long as the intercepts, a, are the same for the different regions, but not necessarily otherwise.

[1] A.P. Thirlwall, 'Types of unemployment, with special reference to "non-demand-deficient" unemployment in the UK', *Scottish Journal of Political Economy*, vol. 16, no. 1, February 1969.

CHAPTER THREE

THE EMPIRICAL RELATION BETWEEN UNEMPLOYMENT AND VACANCY STATISTICS

If unemployment and vacancies in a region are plotted against each other over some periods (of which 1962–5 is one) it is found that they do, in fact, tend to lie on a curve which slopes downwards and is convex to the origin. If both variables are measured logarithmically the relationship is generally negative and linear.[1] The fact that the relationship is of this form is best brought out if all regions are plotted together. The actual observations in any region, or in the country as a whole, lie on quite a small segment of the curve, so that for any single region the fit is not much improved by treating the two variables logarithmically, as table 5 shows. The mean improvement in R^2 from a logarithmic equation is 0·088, that is the explanation of the variation is increased by only 8·8 per cent. But correlation of the improvement in R^2 and the variance of log U for the region yields a positive relationship with $R^2 = 0·905$, which is significant on a t test at 0·1 per cent. This confirms the hypothesis that the bigger the proportionate variation in unemployment rates in a region the more clearly the relationship between unemployment and vacancies is curvilinear, as the theoretical considerations that were mentioned earlier would suggest.[2]

Table 5. *Correlations of unemployment rates and vacancy rates, 1962–5*

	Linear equation		Log. equation		Improvement in R^2
	R	SE	R	SE	
North	−0·868*	±0·062	−0·941*	±0·029	0·132
Yorks. and Lincs.	−0·904*	±0·053	−0·926*	±0·041	0·040
North West	−0·929*	±0·034	−0·971*	±0·014	0·080
Midlands	−0·855*	±0·078	−0·980*	±0·011	0·229
London and South East	−0·920*	±0·038	−0·959*	±0·020	0·074
East and South	−0·879*	±0·057	−0·946*	±0·026	0·122
South West	−0·841*	±0·073	−0·874*	±0·059	0·057
Wales	−0·837	±0·074	−0·857	±0·066	0·033
Scotland	−0·882	±0·056	−0·897	±0·049	0·025

SOURCES: as table 2.

Notes: (i) Quarterly data for all employees, seasonally unadjusted, January 1962 to March 1965.

(ii) An asterisk (*) indicates significance at the 5 per cent level.

[1] In most of this paper, instead of absolute numbers of unemployed and vacancies, numbers of each (seasonally unadjusted) are expressed as a percentage of the region's workforce (male or female as appropriate) to give unemployment rates and vacancy rates. This makes it possible to compare the situation in different regions.

[2] Thirlwall, in 'Types of unemployment', fits arithmetically linear functions to similar data. This is likely to introduce considerable errors into estimates of the points where $U = V$ if the relation is in fact curvilinear, as we have argued, especially where the points in question lie on an extrapolated portion of the line, outside the range of the available data.

These remarks, however, relate to statistics for all employees. It is better to treat the sexes separately. The fact that a significant proportion of women losing their jobs do not register as unemployed naturally means that their rate of registered unemployment is very much lower; it was also declining relative to that of men throughout most of the 1960s.[1] The lower unemployment rate for women than for men is not, however, simply a statistical phenomenon, it also reflects differences in demand. This point is demonstrated by the relationship between vacancies for men and for women as a proportion of number in the labour force. The female vacancy rate is much higher than that for men, and if allowance could be made for the suspected lower notification rate of female vacancies, then the differences in demand would probably be even greater. Moreover, the labour markets for men and for women are very largely separate, with little direct substitution of one sex for the other in jobs of a given description in the short run. A situation in which there is, say, a surplus of male labour but a shortage of female, though it is formally similar to one that we should unhesitatingly characterise as structural unemployment, is best treated as a different kind. We shall accordingly treat the two markets as separate.

The results of the separate analysis for men and for women of the relationship between unemployment and vacancies in each region are set out in table 6. For each region the point where $U = V$ was estimated by regressing recorded unemployment rates on the corresponding vacancy rates, both expressed in logarithms. The constant b can be regarded as an elasticity and, at the point where $U = V$ $(U/V = 1)$, measures the absolute rate of change of U on V. In all cases b is negative, and in most numerically less than unity. The further it is from zero, the more responsive unemployment is to a change in the demand for labour.

There is quite a close relation between regional values of b and mean regional levels of unemployment. For men, R^2 between the two variables is 0·736, significant at the 1 per cent level, for women it is 0·755. The value of R^2 is, however, even higher between the regional values of b and non-demand-deficiency unemployment, estimated at the point $U = V$: for men only a little higher at 0·778, but for women much higher at 0·908. As was noted earlier, these two rival indicators of labour-market inefficiency are not independent of one another.

The regressions of log U on log V have high R^2s generally, but in six out of the nine regions are lower for women than for men – in Scotland, at 0·253, very much lower. On a t test they are all significant at the 0·1 per cent level, except that for women in Scotland which is only just significant at 2 per cent. The period in question thus seems, on the face of it, to be one during which the relation between U and V did not shift greatly in most regions.

The results of the analysis suggest that the regions were divided roughly into three groups: the most efficient labour markets were the Midlands, London and the South East, and Yorkshire and Lincolnshire, where non-demand-deficiency unemployment averaged

---

[1] The difference between registered unemployment rates for men and for women in conjunction with the difference in female activity rates between regions, (see J.K. Bowers, *The Anatomy of Regional Activity Rates*, NIESR Regional Papers I, Cambridge University Press, 1970) might appear to offer at least a partial explanation of differences in overall unemployment rates between regions. But, if the sex ratios of regional labour forces are standardised to the sex ratio for Great Britain and regional sex unemployment ratios are applied, the greatest differences between the standardised and actual unemployment rates is only 0·09 per cent, in the North. The lower overall unemployment rates for the Midlands and the South East, for instance, are explained to only a very small extent by the high proportion of women in their workforces.

Table 6. *The relationship between regional unemployment and vacancy rates,[a] 1962–5*

	Regression coefficients[b]			Non-demand-deficiency unemployment[c]	Actual unemployment[d]
	a	b	R^2	%	%
Males					
North	1·7742	−0·4658	0·746	1·62	3·52
Yorks. and Lincs.	1·6073	−0·6037	0·826	1·01	1·60
North West	1·7337	−0·5636	0·878	1·28	2·33
Midlands	1·7322	−0·8117	0·951	0·90	1·31
London & South East	1·7254	−0·6953	0·834	1·04	1·28
East and South	1·8779	−0·7515	0·794	1·18	1·33
South West	1·8679	−0·7131	0·674	1·23	1·74
Wales	1·7490	−0·4020	0·579	1·77	2·67
Scotland	1·7898	−0·4618	0·743	1·68	3·75
Females					
North	1·7408	−0·5905	0·672	1·24	1·99
Yorks. and Lincs.	1·6312	−0·7426	0·769	0·86	0·81
North West	2·1197	−1·0345	0·803	1·10	1·26
Midlands	1·9144	−1·1317	0·947	0·79	0·72
London & South East	1·8369	−0·9709	0·893	0·86	0·55
East and South	1·9079	−0·9811	0·845	0·92	0·65
South West	1·9396	−0·8627	0·684	1·10	1·05
Wales	1·6153	−0·3656	0·534	1·52	2·02
Scotland	1·6712	−0·3502	0·253	1·73	2·46

SOURCES: as table 2.

[a] Quarterly data for wholly unemployed adults. March 1962 omitted for all regions and June, September and December 1965 for the Midlands and Yorks. and Lincs.

[b] Equation of the form $\log(10\,U) = \log a + b\,\log(10\,V)$. All coefficients are significant at the 1 per cent level.

[c] Estimated at the point $U = V$.

[d] Arithmetic mean over the period.

about 1 per cent of the male labour force and about 0·80 per cent of the female labour force. There was an intermediate group of the South West and the North West, where levels for men and for women were about 1·25 per cent and 1·10 per cent respectively. The most inefficient labour markets were in the high-unemployment regions, the North, Wales and Scotland, where the structural and frictional unemployment of men was estimated at about 1·70 per cent and of women at about 1·50 per cent, although the last figure covers a relatively wide spread from 1·24 per cent in the North to 1·73 per cent in Scotland, with the estimate for Scotland particularly open to question. The remaining region, the East and South, seems to fall between the lowest group and the intermediate group, tending towards the intermediate group for men and the low group for women. For men the spread of non-demand-deficiency unemployment between the most efficient region, the Midlands, and the least efficient, Wales, was almost 0·90 per cent, that is the level was almost twice as high in Wales as in the Midlands. The spread for women was roughly the same.

A considerable amount of work has been done on the more recent relation between unemployment and vacancy statistics for adult males. Initially, the period 1966–7 was investigated, but it subsequently became clear that this was a time in which the relation shifted strongly. The behaviour of the relation for the country as a whole over the period 1959–72 is discussed by Bowers, Cheshire, Webb and Weeden,[1] who find that there seem to have been two sub-periods for which fairly close and convincing relations held – from the third quarter of 1963 to the second of 1966, and from the third quarter of 1969 to the third of 1971.[2] (It seems that, in the first year of the period 1962–5 previously examined, the relation may have been moving slightly inwards towards the origin, but the extent of this shift is not sufficient to invalidate the general indications of the results obtained on the assumption that the relation was unmoved.) The indication is that, while the schedule for U and V had virtually the same elasticity in both periods, it had shifted outwards from the origin by a very considerable amount in the second. (We shall return later to this shift.) The level at which unemployment and unfilled vacancies would have been equal with the relation between them as it was in 1969–71 is a purely hypothetical figure, since the variables were far away from this level. For what it is worth, one can calculate that the point at which $U = V$ moved up from 1·25 per cent to 1·84 per cent.

An earlier article examined the regional unemployment and vacancy data from December 1958 to March 1970,[3] allowing for the shift that began in 1966 by inserting a dummy variable which took the value of zero before the third quarter of that year and unity afterwards. In comparison with the calculation in the later article just mentioned, this suffered from the lack of data for subsequent years. It did, however, yield an estimate for the country as a whole of the pre-1966 point at which unemployment equalled vacancies which was almost identical with that in the later article, and its estimate of the post-1966 point, 1·61, was not so widely different from the later estimate of 1·84 as to destroy confidence in the regional estimates for the period after 1966 as, at any rate, broad indicators of orders of magnitude. They are summarised in table 7. From this it will be seen that the simple estimate of non-demand-deficiency unemployment for the period before 1966, based on equality of U and V, varied from about 1 per cent in London and the South East and the Central region, to about 1·8 per cent in Scotland and Wales (results closely in accordance with those of the previous calculation for 1962–5), while for the $3\frac{1}{2}$ years after the autumn of 1966, the estimate varied from about $1\frac{1}{2}$ per cent in the South Eastern and Central regions to about $2\frac{1}{2}$ per cent in Scotland, Wales and the North whereas actual male unemployment rates in this period varied from about $2\frac{1}{4}$ per cent in the South East to about 5 per cent in Scotland, Wales and the North. Interregional differences in non-demand-deficiency rates were thus between a third and half of those in actual rates of male unemployment. This is about the same proportion as is to be seen in estimates for the years before 1966.

It must be repeated that these calculations rest on the assumption that unemployment and vacancy statistics underestimate the true totals of involuntary worklessness and unfilled vacancies to about the same extent, and that they also depend in most cases on the extrapolation of the empirical relationship between them to values outside the actual

[1] J.K. Bowers, P.C. Cheshire, A.E. Webb and R. Weeden, 'Some aspects of unemployment and the labour market, 1966–71', *National Institute Economic Review*, no. 62, November 1972, pp. 75–88.

[2] There is an indication that there was a further, or continued, shift extending at least to the last quarter of 1972.

[3] J.K. Bowers, P.C. Cheshire and A.E. Webb, 'The change in the relationship between unemployment and earnings increases: a review of some possible explanations', *National Institute Economic Review*, no. 54, November 1970, pp. 44–63.

Table 7.   *Non-demand-deficiency unemployment*[a]

	At point $U = V$		At point $U = 3V$	
	Dec. 1958– June 1966	Sept. 1966– Mar. 1970	Dec. 1958– June 1966	Sept. 1966– Mar. 1970
North	1·66	2·57	2·28	3·54
North West	1·28	1·64	1·90	2·45
Central	1·05	1·51	1·67	2·41
London & South East	1·02	1·42	1·52	2·10
East and South	1·19	1·56	1·91	2·52
South West	1·44	2·07	1·91	2·74
Wales	1·83	2·42	2·50	3·30
Scotland	1·82	2·38	2·44	3·19
Great Britain	1·23	1·61	1·90	2·49

Percentages

SOURCE: NIESR estimates.

[a] Estimates for adult males.

anges experienced in the periods in question. It is possible that the vacancy statistics underestimate what they purport to show to a greater extent than the unemployment statistics do, and it would, in any case, be more satisfactory if the crucial relation between U and V lay within the range of experience in the period in question, or at least not too far outside it. Calculation of the level at which the published unemployment rate would (according to our relation) be three times the published vacancy rate may be regarded as making a rather liberal provision for possible relative under-recording of vacancies, and also brings us into, or nearer to, the range of actual experience – within it for the more prosperous regions before 1966, and near it for the same regions afterwards.

These results are also given in table 7. They give higher estimates of non-demand-deficiency unemployment (if that is what they are thought of as providing), running from a little over 1½ to about 2½ per cent before the 1966 shift, and from a little over 2 to about 3½ per cent thereafter. The range of estimated non-demand-deficiency levels is still between half and a third of the range of actual regional unemployment rates. Interregional variations in the imperfection of labour markets thus estimated still account for only a minor part of interregional unemployment differences, and this is true both before and after the shift that started in 1966.

CHAPTER FOUR

STRUCTURAL AND FRICTIONAL UNEMPLOYMENT

If it is accepted that the level of non-demand-deficiency unemployment is a useful measure of the imperfection of regional labour markets, it becomes interesting to see how far this level in a given region is attributable to frictional and to structural unemployment. The analysis into these two components is straightforward only where there are recorded figures for unemployment and vacancies, by occupation or industry, at or near the point where total unemployment equals total vacancies. Such observations for men exist only in four regions — London and the South East, the East and South, Yorkshire and Lincolnshire, and the Midlands; for women the position is rather better, with relevant observations for seven regions. The following calculations have therefore been limited to the data for women; the resulting regional estimates for 1962—5 are shown in table 8. The components were calculated arithmetically according to the definitions set out on pages 12—13 above, using extrapolation or interpolation as necessary. That is to say, frictional unemployment was calculated as the sum, for all occupational groups, of unemployment or vacancies whichever is the smaller. Structural unemployment is whichever is the smaller of (a) the sum of the excesses of vacancies over unemployment in all the groups where there is such an excess; or (b) the sum of the excesses of unemployment over vacancies in the remaining occupational groups.

Table 8.   *Components of non-demand-deficiency unemployment for women, 1962—5*

	Non-demand-deficiency unemployment[a]	Structural unemployment	*Percentages* Frictional unemployment
North	1·24	0·42	0·82
Yorks. and Lincs.	0·86	0·33	0·53
North West	1·10	0·38	0·72
Midlands	0·79	0·29	0·50
London and South East	0·86	0·18	0·68
East and South	0·92	0·22	0·70
South West	1·10	0·30	0·80
Wales	1·52	0·47	1·05
Scotland[b]	1·73	0·45	1·28

SOURCE: NIESR estimates.

[a] Estimated at the point $U = V$.

[b] The equation in table 6 used to estimate total non-demand-deficiency unemployment was a very poor fit for Scotland; the relationship appeared both to have changed over time and to involve unemployment lagging behind vacancies. From a scatter diagram the relationship seems to have changed at the beginning of the period, indeed just omitting the first two points increases R^2 from 0·253 to 0·625 and reduces the estimate of non-demand-deficiency unemployment to 1·41 per cent. Using all the observations but introducing vacancies lagged one quarter as an additional variable, gives an equation $\log U_t = 4 \cdot 068 - 1 \cdot 384 \log V_t - 0 \cdot 979 \log V_{t-1}$, with $R^2 = 0 \cdot 547$.

Various other approaches would have been possible for regions where there are no data for the range in which unemployment equals vacancies. The distribution of unemployment and vacancies between occupations at the nearest level of unemployment could have been used to derive structural and frictional unemployment arithmetically, but the necessary assumption that the distribution of unemployment and vacancies between occupations is constant does not seem very safe for anything but small movements in their totals in the light of an inspection of the data. It would also be possible to plot the proportion of unemployment (or vacancies) in each category for each region against total unemployment (or vacancies) to give the proportions that go with non-demand-deficiency unemployment by extrapolation or interpolation. Subject to the usual hazards, such as time-trends or permanent shifts in the structure of unemployment or vacancies, this would probably be the best that could be done. It would, however, be very laborious and might not be worth the effort, since for practical purposes the most important distinction is between demand-deficiency unemployment and the rest.

To return, however, to the results shown in table 8. At the outset, one must make some reservations. First the recorded unemployment and vacancy statistics for women bear a more tenuous relationship to reality than those for men. As long as there are no great differences in the accuracy of the figures between regions however, interregional comparisons should have some significance. Secondly, since structural and frictional unemployment in total are defined as equal to non-demand-deficiency unemployment, the greater the possible error in that estimate, the more liable to error will be estimates of the two components. This should be borne in mind particularly for women in Scotland (see the footnote to table 8) and in Wales, where the relations between U and V are poor.

The information in the table suggests some tentative conclusions. London and the South East appears to have the lowest structural unemployment and Wales the highest. The East and South, the South West, the Midlands, Yorkshire and Lincolnshire, and possibly Scotland were intermediate; the North and the North West rather higher, but lower than Wales. Frictional unemployment seemed lowest in Yorkshire and Lincolnshire and the Midlands, with an intermediate group composed of London and the South East, the East and South, and possibly the South West and the North. The highest levels were in Scotland and Wales.

These then were the rather tentative orders of magnitude of the components of unemployment for a period in the middle or late 1960s. The next question is whether these components have anything more than a purely definitional meaning. If these diagnostic categories of unemployment have any connection with the realities of the labour market one might expect differences in their magnitude to be related to identifiable features of the labour market concerned.[1]

An article by G. Davies suggested that for a prospective employer wanting to recruit a labour force, the unemployment rate in an area was not the appropriate measure of the area's available labour supply, what was more important was the absolute numbers unemployed 'within a reasonable travel to work distance'.[2] The implication of this

[1] These could be differences between the regional labour market of a country, differences between subregional labour markets, differences between countries' labour markets, or even inter-temporal differences within the same labour market.

[2] G. Davies, 'Regional unemployment, labour availability and redeployment', *Oxford Economic Papers*, vol. 19, no. 1, March 1967, p. 59.

argument is that, in so far as the movement of enterprises to areas of easy labour supply is a significant part of the adjusting mechanism whereby the unemployed are absorbed into employment, one should be able to observe that this movement is checked at higher percentage levels of unemployment in sparsely populated areas or isolated small communities than in great aggregations of population. If the marginal mobile establishment that decides *not* to move into a particular place were deterred by there being just less than some critical, absolute, number of people available for employment within daily travelling distance, then this number would clearly form a higher proportion of the total labour force in a sparsely than in a densely populated area. This could leave sparsely populated areas with some unemployment that by our criteria would be in the demand-deficiency category, as well as a higher level of structural and frictional unemployment than populous places. So far as structural unemployment alone is concerned, one could argue more simply that the geographical imperfection of the labour market is less when the typical unemployed person is near to a great many workplaces than when he is near to only a few.

At the simplest, regional, level of discussion, it looks as if there may be something in this. It is clear that the most sparsely inhabited British regions, Scotland, Wales, and the North, are the ones with both the highest unemployment rates and the highest calculated values for $U = V$. At the other end of the scale matters are not so straightforward; London and the South East and the West Midlands show the lowest unemployment rates and values for $U = V$, along with high population densities, and the South West and the East and South show slightly higher ones, but the North West, with a high density, shows unemployment rates and values for $U = V$ well above those of the southern half of England.

Labour-market imperfections are obviously too complex to be explained by anything as simple as general, regional, population density — similar values of which may result from many topographical configurations with quite different labour-market implications. So far as the level of unemployment is concerned, it is easy to test its variations with size of community across those towns and development districts for which the rates were separately published, assuming for the purpose that the amounts of labour commuting inward and outward are not so large as to upset altogether the relation under examination. The test cannot be made for all towns and districts for which employment and unemployment is listed in the *Ministry of Labour Gazette* since in non-Development Areas information is given only for the principal towns; and, even there, there is no information for individual exchange areas. To take information for all the towns and districts listed would, therefore, result in a biased sample, since small areas in the low-unemployment regions would be excluded. Confining the analysis to the principal towns and districts within those regions which include Development Areas (with the exception of Yorkshire and Humberside despite the presence in that region of Bridlington) may partially overcome this objection.

Nearly all employment and unemployment data for five regions — the South West, the North West, the North, Scotland and Wales were included. The unemployment rate at a particular date (May 1966) for each district and town in these regions was correlated against total employment in the corresponding area. In all there were 120 towns and districts, and the resultant correlation coefficient had the expected sign and was significant on a t test at the 1 per cent level. The value of R was -0.272 and of R^2 0.074. Thus, for these areas at that date, the absolute size of the labour force of an area xplained 7·4 per cent of the variance in unemployment rates.

As a test of the hypothesis that the smaller the labour force in a labour catchment area the higher will be that area's unemployment rate, this correlation is open to serious objections. First, there is no necessary relationship between labour catchment areas and development districts and principal towns; secondly, both non-demand-deficiency and demand-deficiency unemployment in an area will vary with many other factors besides the one under discussion. Variables for these other factors should, in principle, be included. The *a priori* presumption that a geographically dispersed labour force is one source of labour-market imperfection does, however, receive some empirical support.

CHAPTER FIVE

THE SHIFTING OF THE UNEMPLOYMENT-VACANCY CURVE

The level of regional non-demand-deficiency unemployment (or non-demand-deficiency unemployment in any other area for that matter) has been estimated in the discussion so far from the relation over time between unemployment and vacancies in the region in question. The relation has been estimated by regressing the logarithm of vacancies (expressed as a percentage of the regional labour force) against the logarithm of the unemployment rate in the region. However, whilst equations of this form provided reasonably high R^2s, clearly if the results are to have any economic application, the assumption that the relationship between $\log U$ and $\log V$ is stable over time has to be justified. The original American interest in structural and frictional unemployment developed as a result of an increasing level of unemployment over time, that is their interest was not so much in interregional as in inter-temporal unemployment differences, which is rather at odds with the assumption of stability over time adopted here. Of more immediate relevance is the experience in Britain since the third quarter of 1966. Unemployment has been at an unusually high level in terms of postwar experience throughout this period, but vacancies have also been quite high. A scatter diagram of unemployment against vacancies shows a considerable movement out to the right and away from the origin. This casts further doubt on the assumption that the relationship between $\log U$ and $\log V$ is stable over time.

In view of this, it becomes desirable to search for some means of explaining changes over time in the relationship between U and V. For instance, a factor which might change the level of frictional unemployment in a labour market has recently been suggested by M.W. Reder:[1] the degree of job 'choosiness' amongst the unemployed or applicant 'choosiness' amongst prospective employers prevailing in the market. The suggestion is that legislative changes introducing, for example, redundancy payments and earnings-related benefits may have affected the attitude of the unemployed, whereas employers for their part may equally have been becoming more selective. Changes in transport, too, might alter the efficiency of labour markets, since we already have some reason to suppose that geographical dispersion is a factor producing inefficiency, but they might generally be expected to work slowly.

Structural unemployment, however, whether defined in terms of skills or industrial structures of labour offered and demanded, might well be subject to quite rapid change. The skill (or industrial) structure of the labour force is always changing; similarly the structure of skills demanded. Structural unemployment will increase if the rate of change of the skill of industrial structure of labour is faster than that at which the labour force can adapt; thus in periods (or areas) of rapidly changing techniques of production, structural unemployment can be expected to appear or to increase.

---

[1] M.W. Reder, 'The theory of frictional unemployment', *Economica*, vol. 36, no. 141, February 1969.

Apart from possible variations in frictional unemployment occasioned by legislative changes, structural unemployment, then, would appear to be the component of non-demand-deficiency unemployment most liable to variation over time. It might be possible to explain to some extent differences in structural unemployment with the help of some indicator of change in the structure of demand for labour.

The index of structural change in employment set out in table 9 was calculated by taking the percentage distribution of employment by industrial order in each year in each region and subtracting the corresponding figure for the previous year. These differences in the industrial distribution of employment between successive pairs of years were then added across industries (regardless of sign) to give an index for that region for that pair of years.[1]

Table 9. *An index of structural change in employment*

								Percentages
	North	North West	Central	S.E. England[a]	South West	Wales	Scotland	Great Britain
1959/60	3·71	2·92	3·90	2·28	2·72	6·09	3·59	2·71
1960/1	3·57	3·15	2·54	1·78	2·40	3·50	3·40	2·18
1961/2	3·29	1·47	2·72	1·41	3·41	3·02	3·37	2·09
1962/3	4·37	2·91	2·28	1·75	2·26	2·94	3·83	2·10
1963/4	5·72	3·36	2·31	2·34	4·28	4·61	3·78	2·68
1964/5	3·36	2·63	2·57	1·39	4·87	4·23	2·80	2·00
1965/6	5·00	2·26	2·62	1·76	2·84	4·59	3·15	2·02
1966/7[b]	4·20	4·88	3·83	3·64	4·17	4·49	3·92	3·66
1967/8	5·31	2·62	2·48	2·49	2·96	4·62	2·72	1·97
Mean	4·28	2·91	2·81	2·09	3·32	4·23	3·40	2·38

SOURCE: tabulations supplied by the Department of Employment and Productivity.

London and South East combined with the East and South owing to boundary changes.

Probably the index was increased in this year by the induced movement into self-employment in construction.

There are a number of reasons why this index might not be the ideal indicator to use as an explanatory variable for structural and frictional unemployment. The only figures available are for a breakdown of employment by region, sex and industry. In as far as industries are geographically concentrated and labour is spatially immobile, one might expect an index derived from an industrial breakdown of employment to provide a degree of explanation of the 'locational' type of frictional unemployment mentioned on page 13. Structural unemployment, on the other hand, one would expect to be related to an index constructed from a breakdown of demand by skills rather than by industry, since labour tends to be skill-specific rather than industry-specific. To some extent, however, the industrial structure does reflect differences in skills; so an index constructed from it will be a useful proxy, but the degree to which this is true varies from industry to industry. In some industries the divisions of the Standard Industrial

On *a priori* grounds, vacancies should be included in the calculation of any index of structural change in the demand for labour. Recorded vacancies are, however, at any time commonly less than 1 per cent of total employment, so their exclusion makes only a small difference to the actual value of the index. In view of this, it seemed better to exclude them, since they are only available by region and industry for a shorter period than statistics of employment.

Classification may be too fine — the division between vehicles and engineering might be an example — in others the division may not be detailed enough — for example, the lack of breakdown between man-made and other textiles, or the combined order of bricks, pottery and glass. Clearly, if industrial change *per se* does have an influence on non-demand-deficiency unemployment, the amount of unemployment for a given change will, at least in part, depend on the industry in which the change occurs. The amount of unemployment resulting from a given change should depend, *ceteris paribus*, on how far labour, for reasons of either location or skill, is specific to the changing industries. Ideally some account should be taken of how specific labour is to each industry, but this, though it might be a useful line of inquiry, is beyond the scope of the present investigation.

Table 10.   *Regional unemployment differences explained by structure of employment and other variables*

	Constant	Vacancy rate (log V_t)	Change in employment structure (E_t)	(E_{t-1})	Linear time-trend	Regional dummies	R^2	S.E.	D.W
1.	0·326 (0·056)	−0·874 (0·089)					0·642	0·301	0·7
2.	−0·159 (0·113)	−0·750* (0·080)	0·166* (0·035)				0·748	0·255	1·2
3.	−0·402* (0·117)	−0·739* (0·071)	0·115* (0·034)	0·126* (0·032)			0·807	0·225	1·0
4.	−0·516* (0·101)	−0·775* (0·059)	0·080* (0·029)	0·113* (0·027)	0·056* (0·012)		0·868	0·188	0·8
5.	−0·208 (0·167)	−0·785* (0·057)	0·026 (0·026)	0·069* (0·024)	0·067 (0·009)	−0·054 (0·084) −0·362* (0·093) −0·069 (0·120) −0·028 (0·084) 0·225* (0·071) 0·035 (0·715)	0·947	0·127	1·7

SOURCES: as tables 1 and 9.

Notes: (i) Standard errors are shown in brackets.
   (ii) An asterisk (*) indicates significance at the 5 per cent level.
   (iii) Regional dummies are for the North West, the Central region, South Eastern England, the South West, Wales and Scotland in that order, with the North as a datum.

With these qualifications of the usefulness of the index of structural change in mind, what results does it give? Table 10 sets out the regression and correlation coefficients obtained from analysing the data for seven British regions individually and together. In each case the logarithm of the unemployment rate is the dependent variable and the logarithm of the vacancy rate the first independent variable. Data, after allowing for the equations involving a lag, were available for eight years (1960—8) and taking all seven regions together this provided 56 observations. As can be seen from equation 1, the level of vacancies by itself explained 64 per cent of the variance in unemployment levels during this period, though the Durbin—Watson statistic, given in the last column, dicates the existence of autocorrelation.

Further equations were then tried, adding as independent variables first E_t, the value
: the index of structural change in employment in the region at time t, that is the change
the structure of employment in a region since the previous year, and second E_{t-1}, the
lue of the index in structural change in employment for one year earlier.

The coefficients for both E_t and E_{t-1} have the expected sign, and including both of
em increases R^2 to 0·807. The equation is, however, unsatisfactory on two counts. The
efficient for E_{t-1} is larger than that for E_t (though by less than the standard error of
ther) whereas *a priori* one would expect changes in the structure of employment in the
riod immediately preceding the observed unemployment to have more effect than
anges during the previous period. Also the Durbin–Watson statistic continues to be
nsatisfactory. Adding a linear time-trend increases R^2 further to 0·868 and all the inde-
endent variables remain significant, but the value of the coefficient for E_t falls relative
to that for E_{t-1} and the Durbin–Watson statistic also falls.

The next step in the analysis was to include a dummy variable for each region. The
ain reason for this was that one might expect differing constant levels of unemployment
: a given level of vacancies and of structural change as a result of differing constant levels
f frictional unemployment between regions. This device (equation 5), with the North
cting as datum, produced significant regional dummy coefficients for only two regions –
positive one for Wales and a negative one for the Central region. Perhaps surprisingly, in
outh Eastern England, although the coefficient had a negative sign, it was comparatively
nall and non-significant. Adding regional dummies increased the R^2 even further to
·947, and the value of the Durbin–Watson statistic moved at least into the upper realms
f indeterminacy; the coefficient for E_t, however, became even smaller compared to that
or E_{t-1} and ceased to be significant.[1]

An attempt was made to analyse the data for the various regions separately in a
milar way. Great caution is necessary in interpreting this, since there are only eight obser-
ations for each region. The result is that, despite the paucity of degrees of freedom, all
ie explanatory variables – vacancies, unlagged structural change, lagged structural change
nd a time-trend – seem to have been significant in the South East; that in the North West
ll of these except unlagged structural change were significant; but in the Central region,
ie North and Scotland, only vacancies and the time-trend attained this status; whilst in
Vales and the South West none of the variables attained the 5 per cent significance level.
'he general impression left by this is that change in industrial structure is an explanatory
ariable that helps in explaining unemployment levels, but that it does not help everywhere.

Perhaps the most significant deficiency in these various attempts to explain regional
nemployment rates is the under-explanation of the rise in unemployment relative to va-
ancies in the last two years of the period, 1967 and 1968. It would seem that the obvious
ne of further enquiry is to seek a variable for other factors which might have changed
uddenly in these later years.

Two such changes have been cited as possible factors in the increase in unemploy-
nent relative to vacancies in the late 1960s; redundancy payments, which came into force

As noted in a footnote to table 9, the movement into self-employment in construction might have
ffected the value of the index of structural change in employment in 1966/7 and perhaps in other
ears. Accordingly the index was recalculated excluding construction and the full set of regressions
vas run using these values. The results, however, were very little different to those reported in table
0 and on the whole slightly less satisfactory.

in December 1965, and earnings-related unemployment benefit, which began to be paid in October 1966. Both changes might be seen as increasing frictional unemployment – making people more willing to stay out of work by increasing their 'choosiness'. Thus, for any given level of job-opportunities as indicated by unfilled vacancies, there might be more out of work, or, at any given unemployment level, more unfilled vacancies. The obvious way in which a change in legislation can be allowed for is by introducing a dummy variable for the appropriate years. Two attempts of this kind have been made. The first used, once more, the data for all regions together, with and without regional and various policy dummies; the second took the data separately for each region. The results of the first of these attempts are shown in table 11.

Table 11. *Regional unemployment differences explained by structure of employment, policy dummies and other variables*

	Constant	Vacancy ratio (log V_t)	Change in employment structure (E_t)	(E_{t-1})	Linear time-trend	Policy dummies (d_1)	(d_2)	Regional dummies	R^2	S.E.
1.	−0·478* (0·108)	−0·777* (0·060)	0·080* (0·029)	0·114* (0·027)	0·039* (0·021)	0·094 (0·098)			0·870	0·189
2.	−0·412* (0·111)	−0·743* (0·061)	0·081* (0·028)	0·111* (0·026)	0·024 (0·021)	0·030 (0·101)	0·184* (0·096)		0·879	0·184
3.	0·270* (0·145)	−0·641* (0·058)	0·014 (0·021)	0·043* (0·021)		0·071 (0·050)	0·343* (0·063)	−0·156* (0·062) −0·504* (0·073) −0·287* (0·101) −0·173* (0·070) 0·133* (0·058)	0·960	0·110
4.	0·328* (0·141)	−0·608* (0·054)	0·014 (0·021)	0·038 (0·021)			0·411* (0·041)	−0·172* (0·062) −0·529* (0·072) −0·326* (0·098) −0·201* (0·068) 0·115* (0·057)	0·958	0·112
5.	0·207* (0·136)	−0·657* (0·054)	0·004 (0·020)	0·037 (0·020)	0·035* (0·012)	−0·029 (0·058)	0·292* (0·061)	−0·165* (0·058) −0·512* (0·068) −0·300* (0·094) −0·168* (0·065) 0·145* (0·054)	0·966	0·102

SOURCES: as tables 1 and 9.

Notes: (i) Standard errors are shown in brackets.
(ii) An asterisk (∗) indicates significance at the 5 per cent level.
(iii) Regional dummies in each equation are for the North West, the Central region, South East England, the South West and Wales in that order, with the North and Scotland combined as a datum.

Perhaps the most interesting conclusion to emerge is how relatively insignificant this departure was. Comparing equation 2 in table 11 with equation 4 in table 10, it will be seen that adding a dummy of both earnings-related payments (d_2) and redundancy payments (d_1) adds only 0·01 to the value of R^2 and d_1 (for 1966, 1967 and 1968) is not significant, whilst d_2 (1967 and 1968) is only barely significant at twice its standard error. In contrast, the coefficients for E_t and E_{t-1} are three and four times their standard errors.

However, as was the case with the analyses listed in table 10, it would seem that a major element in the explanatory powers of E_t and E_{t-1} is in accounting for differences in unemployment between regions. When regional dummies are added (this time Scotland and the North acted jointly as datum, a step necessitated by terminal capacity) then, as before, the coefficient for E_t is reduced in value and ceases to be significant, whilst that for E_{t-1} is reduced in value and becomes only intermittently significant. The dummy for redundancy payments is not significant in any equation and indeed, in equation 5 where all variables are included, has a negative sign. Therefore it does not seem worth discussing this further. The dummy for earnings-related payments has the expected positive sign and is significant, but it does not eliminate the significance of the time-trend. The other major difference between this equation and the corresponding one, equation 5, in table 10 is that including a dummy for 1967 and 1968 makes the regional dummies much larger and more of them appear significant; also, the coefficients for E_t and E_{t-1} are reduced in size. In effect this means that more of the differences between regional unemployment levels are being left unexplained.

In the equations that were calculated for the individual regions, it appeared that a dummy for the last two years of the period (representing earnings-related benefit) was less successful than a simple time-trend. Five of the coefficients for a simple time-trend were significant, compared with only two of the coefficients for the shift dummy; and more of the coefficients for the other variables also tended to be significant in equations using a simple time-trend.

Very broadly, then, the conclusion is that a dummy variable inserted to represent an immediate effect of redundancy payments does no significant good, whilst one put in to stand for immediate effects of earnings-related benefits does not improve the relation much over and above what can be achieved by a simple time-trend. The upward movement of unemployment for given values of the other variables in the later years of the period was of a different extent in different regions. In conjunction with the later work on the shifts of the unemployment—vacancy curve which has already been mentioned, this suggests that if either or both of the two legislative changes under discussion made a substantial difference to the apparent 'imperfection' of regional labour markets, they did not do so all at once, but over a period of years; also they operated either at rather different rates in different regions, or to the accompaniment of influences peculiar to particular regions that in varying degrees masked or accentuated their effects. None of this, of course, is at all improbable *a priori*, but further work using more recent data would be required to support it, and such support could never, of course, in the nature of things, provide ground for certainty.

It seems fairly clear that, according to the criteria adopted here, regional labour markets and the labour market of the country as a whole did become markedly more imperfect after 1966, but the reasons for this must remain to a large extent conjectural. The important conclusion that our analysis here suggests very strongly is that, both before and after the changes just mentioned, those differences between regional unemployment levels that can be plausibly attributed to interregional differences in labour-market imper fections have been very decidedly smaller than those that cannot be thus attributed. Differences in demand pressure seem to account for the major part of interregional differences in actual unemployment levels.

THE MINISTRY OF LABOUR SURVEY OF THE
CHARACTERISTICS OF THE UNEMPLOYED

This paper has set out to examine regional differences in unemployment; how far and how directly such differences can be traced to the varying industrial structures of the regions; how far they can be attributed simply to differences in demand for labour in different regions of the country, or alternatively to different levels of non-demand-deficiency unemployment. Finally, consideration has been given to possible causes of regional differences in the components of non-demand-deficiency unemployment — structural and frictional unemployment. It might seem at first sight that an ideal source of information for this study would have been a survey of the characteristics of the un-employed. Since such a survey exists — the Ministry of Labour survey of the character-stics of the unemployed — it might seem surprising that no use has been made of it.[1]

The reason, in brief, is that neither the characteristics of the unemployed nor the assessments made of most of those characteristics are likely to be independent of the pressure of demand for labour. This makes it hard to interpret such assessments to throw light on differences in the causes of unemployment in different regions between which the pressure of demand varies. The subject, however, requires further attention.

The survey was based on a 10 per cent sample of the unemployed registered on 12 October 1964.[2] The survey, which is available on a regional basis, classified the un-employed by a wide range of characteristics, including sex, age and prospects of securing employment. It is this last classification in which we are most interested for the purposes of the present paper.

The unemployed in each region were classified into one of four categories:
  (a) should get work without difficulty;
  (b) will find difficulty in getting work because of lack of local opportunity;
  (c) will find difficulty in getting work because qualifications, experience or degree of skill in occupation for which registered unacceptable to employers;
  (d) will find difficulty in getting work on personal grounds (for example, age, prison record, lack of English, non-member of trade union).

In principle, this last group — those likely to find difficulty in getting work on personal grounds — are included in the structural and frictional unemployed we have already iden-tified; thus, this independent assessment of their regional variation should be most valuable.

These 'difficult to place',[3] like the structural and frictional unemployed, might be

---

[1] A summary of the results of this survey appeared in the *Ministry of Labour Gazette* for April and July 1966. This appendix is based on the full tabulations which the Ministry of Labour kindly made available to us.

[2] There was also an earlier survey carried out in August 1961.

[3] This term, in inverted commas, is used throughout to cover the unemployed classified in the survey as likely to 'find difficulty in getting work on personal grounds'.

liable to remain out of work even if demand-deficiency unemployment had been eliminated. There were two other categories in the tabulations which might have contained some of the non-demand-deficiency unemployed – under (b)[1] and (c) above – who might be classed as 'structural' unemployed. However, although there might have been variations from region to region, it would seem reasonable to assume that those difficult to place for lack of local opportunity would have been mainly demand-deficiency unemployed, and that the category of those with qualifications unacceptable to employers was so small a percentage of the national labour force (0·022) that they, too, could be ignored.

This conclusion, that there is a measure of comparability between the structural and frictional unemployed and those 'difficult to place on personal grounds', is similar to that implicit in Professor Paish's attempts to identify regional 'non-effective' unemployment.[2] 'Non-effective unemployment' he defined as people now classified as unemployed who suffer from various personal disabilities which make them 'likely to spend long periods on the register even when local demand is high'.[3] These people '... cannot be regarded as competing effectively for the vacancies available'.[4] From the Ministry of Labour survey Professor Paish concluded that there were 'over 180,000 non-effective unemployed in Great Britain in October 1964, that is those classified in the tabulations as likely to find difficulty in getting work on personal grounds.

How, then, do our estimates of structural and frictional unemployed and the 'difficult to place' as estimated by the Ministry of Labour (Professor Paish's 'non-effective' unemployed) in fact compare? The number of unemployed men and women classified as likely to find difficulty in getting work on personal grounds, the percentage they formed of the regional labour force and our estimates of structural and frictional unemployment for the period 1961–5 are set out in table A.1.

To test for an association between the number of 'difficult to place' in a region and our estimates of structural and frictional unemployment, six across-region correlations were done, three for men and three for women. The number of 'difficult to place' expressed as a percentage of the regional labour force was correlated against our estimates of structural and frictional unemployment in the region, the 'difficult to place' rate was correlated with the overall unemployment rate in the region at the time of the survey and our estimates of structural and frictional unemployment were correlated against the mean quarterly unemployment rate in the region in the period 1961–5.

The results of these correlations for men and women are set out in table A.2, which shows that there is indeed a clear and highly significant relationship between our structural and frictional rates and the 'difficult to place' rate in a region. R^2 is 0·84 for men and 0·79 for women. From table A.1, however, it will be seen that the estimate of 'difficult to place' derived from the Ministry of Labour survey tends to be lower than our structural and frictional unemployment in the low-unemployment regions but, for men at least, slightly higher in the high-unemployment regions. Taking the 'difficult to place' rate as the dependent variable, the estimated value of b is 0·97 for women ($a = -0·55$) and 1·49 for men ($a = -0·81$).

[1] This category might include some 'locational' frictional unemployment.

[2] F.W. Paish, 'How the economy works', *Lloyds Bank Review*, April 1968, pp. 1–31.

[3] *Ministry of Labour Gazette*, April 1966.

[4] Paish, 'How the economy works'.

Table A.1.   *'Difficult to place' and estimated structural and frictional unemployment, 1961–6*

	Males			Females		
	'Difficult to place'		Structural and frictional unemploy-ment	'Difficult to place'		Structural and frictional unemploy-ment
	Numbers	Proportion of labour force		Numbers	Proportion of labour force	
	000s	%	%	000s	%	%
North	16·63	*1·89*	*1·62*	4·30	*1·00*	*1·24*
Yorks. & Lincs.	10·95	*0·75*	*1·01*	2·65	*0·34*	*0·86*
North West	23·31	*1·24*	*1·28*	6·78	*0·59*	*1·10*
Midlands	13·86	*0·59*	*0·90*	3·47	*0·27*	*0·79*
London & South East	22·19	*0·62*	*1·04*	5·09	*0·23*	*0·86*
East & South	11·76	*0·71*	*1·18*	2·48	*0·26*	*0·92*
South West	8·71	*1·00*	*1·23*	1·71	*0·27*	*1·10*
Wales	9·99	*1·45*	*1·77*	2·54	*0·82*	*1·52*
Scotland	25·81	*1·85*	*1·68*	9·10	*1·13*	*1·73*
Great Britain	143·21	*0·97*	*n.a.*	38·12	*0·46*	*n.a.*

SOURCE: Ministry of Labour survey.

Table A.2.   *The relationship between non-demand-deficiency unemployment, 'difficult to place' rates and overall unemployment rates, 1961–5*

	Regression coefficients		R^2	t
	a	b		
Male unemployment				
'Difficult to place'/non-demand-deficiency	−0·81	1·49	0·84*	16·65
'Difficult to place'/overall rate, 1964	0·08	0·56	0·99*	307·76
Non-demand-deficiency/mean quarterly rate, 1961–5	0·67	0·29	0·78*	11·88
Female unemployment				
'Difficult to place'/non-demand-deficiency	−0·55	0·97	0·79*	12·45
'Difficult to place'/overall rate, 1964	−0·02	0·49	0·93*	41·83
Non-demand-deficiency/mean quarterly rate, 1961–5	0·57	0·44	0·91*	30·90

SOURCE: NIESR estimates.

Note: An asterisk (*) indicates significance at the 5 per cent level.

However, the most striking relationship in table A.2 is that between the 'difficult to place' rate and the overall unemployment rate across regions. This has an R^2 of 0·99 for men and 0·93 for women; the R^2, particularly for men, is so high that, taken in conjunction with other evidence, it suggests that the number of unemployed classified as 'likely to find difficulty getting work on personal grounds' in a region is not independent of the level of unemployment in that region.[1]

This might be so because of non-uniformity in standards of classification. The Ministry of Labour were aware it would be difficult to ensure that offices in the regions applied the survey classifications objectively; it is clearly difficult to get classifications such as those used in the survey applied with reference to some standard level of demand rather than the regional or even subregional level of demand. In April 1966 the *Ministry of Labour Gazette* summed up the problem as follows:

> It should be noted that answers to some of the questions (e.g. about prospects of finding suitable employment) depended on subjective judgement by the officers completing the forms ... where unemployment is highest ... it seems likely that ... officers have judged personal characteristics to be the main reason for difficulty in placing some men and women who would have found jobs fairly readily elsewhere. Although Local Offices were asked to consider carefully whether registrants would have reasonable prospects of getting work in another area, it is not always easy to do this, particularly in areas where there has persistently been unemployment above the average. This group (i.e. those classified as likely to find difficulty in getting work on personal grounds [the 'difficult to place'] is likely to be somewhat smaller than the survey figures indicate, and the group of people who would have good prospects if local opportunities were greater should be correspondingly larger. Many of them (i.e. those classified as difficult to place on personal grounds) are likely to spend long periods on the register even when local demand for labour is high.[2]

Thus the figure of 180,000 'non-effective' unemployed, which Professor Paish took as a minimum, was seen by the Ministry of Labour as a maximum for October 1964 — indeed a maximum which was almost certainly not reached.

There is, however, a second and probably even more important way in which the level of demand in a region could be expected to influence the number of unemployed in that region judged as 'difficult to place'. Even if the potential employability of a man could be assessed entirely objectively with reference to the national rather than to the purely local state of demand, the actual number of 'difficult to place' observed would almost certainly be dependent on the level of demand in the region. The 'difficult to place' are not a clear-cut class who are all unemployed in all conditions; at any given time, a proportion of them will be in work, and this proportion will be higher where unemployment is low than where it is high.

These two sources of difficulty interact. If the Ministry's standards were completely uniform between regions, and if the characteristics of people relevant to their employability were the same in all regions, one would expect the unemployed to consist more of people inherently difficult to employ and less of people with good qualifications in regions of labour shortage than in those of high unemployment. This carries the implication that, if one looks only at the unemployed (as the Ministry's survey does), the less employable people to be found among them will constitute smaller proportions of the whole working population in regions of labour shortage; in these regions, more of such people will be in employment than where unemployment is high. If the Ministry found a

---

[1] If a multiple correlation is done, taking the 'difficult to place' rate as the dependent variable again, and using the unemployment rate and our estimates of structural and frictional unemployment as the independent variables, the R^2 remains at $0·99$ and the associated regression coefficient with structural and frictional unemployment is totally non-significant with a t value of $0·06$; i.e. the unemployment rate in the region 'explains' all the variation in the 'difficult to place' rate between regions.

[2] This point has also been made in D.J. Mackay, 'Regional policy and labour reserves in Scotland – II' *Journal of Economic Studies*, vol. 3, no. 1, March 1968.

igher proportion of the unemployed 'hard to place on personal grounds' in regions of igh unemployment, one might conclude either that these regions really do contain higher roportions of such people in their populations, or that the Ministry's standards are influenced by the local demand for labour; it would be hard to assign responsibility between these two potential causes.

In fact, the proportion of the unemployed who were classified as 'difficult to place or personal reasons' did not vary much between regions. It was relatively low in Scotland and high in the Midlands, which produced a significant but low negative correlation $R^2 = 0.35$) with regional unemployment rates. This suggests that there was neither distortion of the classification by the local demand situation, nor interregional differences in the ncidence of the less employable among the working population to any very large extent. That either or both of these conditions prevailed to a small extent, however, remains possible.

Absence of any great distortion of the classification by local demand conditions is suggested by another circumstance. The percentage of those classified as 'difficult to place on account of age' who were over 60 was not significantly correlated with regional unemployment rates (the coefficient, though negative, was non-significant); if the judgement had been strongly influenced by local demand conditions, one would have expected a significant negative correlation − younger men judged too old for work where unemployment was high. On the other hand, the percentage of those classified as: 'difficult to place on account of mental or physical condition' who were cross-classified as 'able-bodied' was significantly correlated with the unemployment rate though not very highly ($R^2 = 0.35$). This suggests some systematic tendency for unemployability to be more inclusively judged where regional unemployment was high, but the tendency cannot have been a very strong one. There remains some doubt about the uniformity of classification, but a presumption that it was not grossly distorted by demand variations.

On the second source of difficulty − the varying distribution between the employed and the unemployed of people who have some definite handicap in finding employment − there is one useful piece of evidence, namely the statistics relating to the registered disabled.

The relevant data on the disabled are set out in table A.3. It is immediately clear that there is a strong positive correlation between columns 4 and 5. R is 0.91 (R^2, 0.84) and t is 16.72, significant at 0.1 per cent. The value of the regression coefficient is 3.37, which suggests that an interregional difference of 1 per cent in the overall unemployment rate goes with a difference in the unemployment rate for the registered disabled of 3.37 per cent. As a group therefore, the registered disabled were marginal workers who were affected by differences in the level of demand more than were other workers, and on whom unemployment everywhere bore disproportionately.

If one moves from considering the unemployment rate of the registered disabled to regional differences in the numbers of unemployed registered disabled in relation to the total regional labour force, then clearly another factor must be involved − that is the total number of registered disabled in the region. A multiple correlation using both the regional unemployment rate and the total number of registered disabled in the region as independent variables yields an R^2 of 0.97 and both variables are significant at the 1 per cent level.

The distribution of the registered disabled has been analysed here because they are the only group of less easily employable workers for which there is information about their existence amongst the employed as well as the unemployed. Also, since they were

39

Table A.3.   *The registered disabled [a] by region, April 1964*

	Registered disabled		Disabled unemployed		Unemploy-ment rate
	Numbers	Proportion of labour force	Numbers	Proportion of registered disabled [b]	
	(1)	(2)	(3)	(4)	(5)
	000s	%	000s	%	%
North	43·76	3·34	5·69	13·00	2·69
Yorks. & Lincs.	72·91	3·27	5·49	7·53	1·01
North West	98·89	3·27	8·31	8·40	1·67
Midlands	102·56	2·82	5·41	5·28	0·71
London & South East	128·16	2·21	6·13	4·78	0·83
East & South	66·10	2·50	3·84	5·81	0·93
South West	38·62	2·90	2·72	7·04	1·42
Wales	40·91	4·11	5·14	12·57	2·23
Scotland	63·98	2·92	6·93	10·83	2·95
Great Britain	655·88	2·83	49·66	7·57	1·35

SOURCES: Department of Employment; *Ministry of Labour Gazette.*

[a] Males and females.

[b] Equivalent to an unemployment rate for the registered disabled.

defined as workers 'substantially handicapped in obtaining or keeping employment' it would seem reasonable to suppose that they were at least to some extent comparable to the category 'difficult to place on personal grounds' used in the survey. So far as this is so it would appear that our second hypothesis tends to be substantiated: that is, the registered disabled, and so by extension one would argue the 'difficult to place', tended to behave like marginal workers rather than 'unemployables'. Consequently the proportion of a region's labour force identified in the survey of the characteristics of the unemployed as 'difficult to place on personal grounds' was as much a function of the unemployment rate in the region as of the number of less easily employable in the region's labour force as a whole.

The conclusion to be drawn from this is that, even if the standards applied in the survey are unaffected by local demand conditions, it still does not provide an assessment of the relative incidences of the personal qualities with which it is concerned among regional labour forces.

Interregional Migration Models and their Application to Great Britain

by R. WEEDEN

INTRODUCTION

The purpose of this study is to explain, with the aid of statistical models of migration, the level and direction of interregional migration in Great Britain for the five-year period 1961–6 and the two one-year periods 1960–1 and 1965–6.

In chapter 1 the basic concepts and definitions of migration research are introduced, with comment on methods of collecting data, their availability and the methodological problems associated with the British Census. The literature on migration models is scattered throughout economic, sociological and demographic journals, and chapter 2 examines the three main types of model used to explain interregional migration – *ad hoc*, gravitational, and Markov chain models. The difference between the models and possible uses of a successful one are considered. Empirical results of a series of *ad hoc* models are given in chapter 3, and chapter 4 presents the results of a covariance model of migration between the subregions of southern England, and of two analysis of variance models which are used to test the significance of changes in the interregional migration pattern between 1960–1 and 1965–6.

CHAPTER ONE

CONCEPTS AND DEFINITIONS

THE MIGRATION-FLOW MATRIX

It will be useful to start with some basic concepts, some of them very familiar and straight forward, but others involving problems that are easily overlooked.

Four distinct demographic processes generate changes in the sizes of regional populations – births, deaths, internal migration and external migration. Internal (or more precisely interregional) migration is the subject of this paper. Initially, the other processes of change are ignored, by considering population flows within a closed system of regions and assuming that the size of the national population is constant.

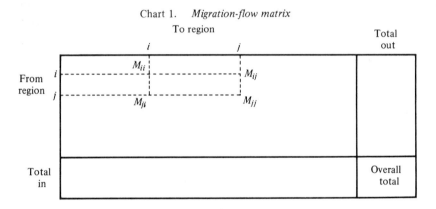

Chart 1. *Migration-flow matrix*

The basic conceptual device for the analysis of interregional migration is the migration-flow matrix shown in chart 1. It is defined for a given time period t and a specified set of regions of a geographical area. Ideally data should be available in the form of a consecutive set of matrices (a time-series of data with each matrix complete). The typical off-diagonal element of the matrix is M_{ij}, the flow of migrants from region i to region j. The problem is to define the diagonal element, M_{ii}. In general there are three possibilities which give different sums of elements by rows, columns and overall (table 1). The table may be augmented by regional vectors of births, deaths, immigrants from abroad and emigrants overseas.

Given the basic information summarised in the migration-flow matrix, further information may be derived:

(a) The net balance, $M_{ji} - M_{ij}$, is the net interchange of migrants between a pair of regions. The alternative to calculating this value is to inspect the 'balance of signs', that is whether $M_{ji} - M_{ij}$ is positive or negative.

atrix	M_{ii}	Row and column totals	Overall total
$_1$	Zero	Emigrants and immigrants for each region	Total interregional migrants
$_2$	Intra-regional migrants	'Movers',[a] in and out	Total 'movers'[a]
$_3$	Non-migrants *plus* intra-regional migrants	Regional populations, at start and at end of period	Total population[b]

Persons changing address.

Assumed constant.

(b) Total attraction or gross interchange, $M_{ji} + M_{ij}$, is the total interchange of migrants between two regions.

(c) Total immigrants to region i from other regions are defined (assuming $M_{ii} = 0$) as the gross flow, $I_i = \Sigma_j M_{ji}$, and total emigrants from region i to other regions are $E_i = \Sigma_j M_{ij}$; therefore net migration into region i from other regions is given by $N_i = I_i - E_i = \Sigma_j (M_{ji} - M_{ij})$ and, because the system is closed, $\Sigma_i N_i = 0$.

How are migration flows measured? In general there are four methods that might e used:[1]

(a) The residual method, under which the observed total change in a regional population during a given period of time is adjusted for (registered) births and deaths to give, as a residual, net internal plus net external migration. Clearly data from this source are likely to be poor in quality, and do not yield information on internal migration unless internal and external migration can be separated.

(b) Direct inquiry gathers information on internal migration by posing the question, 'What was your address n years ago?'. A migrant from region i to region j is defined as a person with an address in region i at the start of the period but in region j at the census date. A person who moves from A to B to C during the period is classified as moving from A to C, and a person who moves from A to B to A is not counted as an interregional migrant at all. But provided the period is not too long such problems of classification should not be too important. Both sets of census data used in this study were gathered by this method.

(c) The 'lifetime' method is similar to direct inquiry, but 'address n years ago' becomes 'place of birth'. Often the only data available are of this type,[2] but the method is inferior to direct inquiry because the time period varies with the age of the migrant and a person moving from A to B to C to D is still classified as moving from A to D.

(d) Under a system of population registration, persons changing address are legally required to notify a central authority. Assuming that people comply speedily

The data at present available are discussed on pp. 46–50 below.

Three recent studies of developing countries use this sort of data: R. Beals, M. Levy and L. Moses, Rationality and migration in Ghana', *Review of Economics and Statistics*, vol. 49, November 1967, p. 480–6; G.S. Sahota, 'An economic analysis of internal migration in Brazil', *Journal of Political Economy*, vol. 76, March–April 1968, pp. 218–45; N.A. Adams, 'Internal migration in Jamaica: an conomic analysis', *Social and Economic Studies*, vol. 18, June 1969, pp. 137–51.

with the law, then the resulting information is free from the problems associate
with previous methods. Few countries adopt this method; a National Register
was operated in this country from September 1939 to February 1952 and two
published studies use this material.[1] There are several other sources that could
give similar information as a by-product, for example, National Health Service
cards[2] or electoral rolls.

Finally, two general points should be emphasised. First, the type of migration
analysed in this paper is residential migration. Change of address does not necessarily
correspond to change of workplace. Secondly, since interregional migration is migration
across interregional boundaries, and its observed level depends on how many boundaries
are drawn, we must beware of statements like the following: 'In the United States ...
annual interstate mobility [affects] about 3% of the population. Annual rates of interregional mobility [are] for Italy, $\frac{1}{2}$%: West Germany 1·8%; and for France, 1·0% ... These
figures suggest that the recent rate of rather more than 2% in England and Wales falls
short of the American rate, but is greater than the rate for a number of other European
countries'.[3]

MIGRATION RATES

It is conventional to calculate migration rates, both net and gross, in the same way as
birth and death rates, that is per thousand of the population. This raises the question of
which measure of population should be used. Ideally one would estimate the number of
persons 'at risk' (exposed to migration from i to j during the given time period). The
normal measure − the population at the census date when information about previous
movements was collected, includes persons not likely to migrate from region i during the
period to which the inquiry relates (very recent immigrants from other regions and from
abroad). So what definition should be used? From an analytical point of view it is reason
able to treat the major demographic processes separately, although the situation in the
real world is not quite so simple. Some people who migrate into an area in the inquiry
period die or move abroad before the census date, others will have been born or will have
arrived from abroad during the inquiry period. In this paper immigrants from abroad and
net internal migrants are subtracted from population at the census date as an approximation to the theoretical ideal.

AVAILABILITY OF THE DATA

There are several sources of data on interregional migration, usefully summarised by

[1] General Register Office, *Internal Migration: some aspects of population movements within England*
and Wales by M.P. Newton and J.R. Jeffery, London, HMSO, 1951 and *Internal Migration: a study o,*
the frequency of movement of migrants by J.A. Rowntree, London, HMSO, 1957.

[2] Used in T.H. Hollingworth, 'Internal migration statistics from the central register for Scotland of
the National Health Service', *Journal of the Royal Statistical Society* (series A), vol. 131, 1968,
pp. 340−80.

[3] *Ministry of Labour Gazette*, August 1967, p. 620. I am indebted to Mr R.J. Van Noorden for
drawing my attention to this comment.

Thompson.[1] The present study is based on the Censuses of 1961 and 1966. Table 2 summarises the available census data on the migration-flow matrix at various levels of aggregation.

Table 2. *Census data available on migration-flows*

	1961[a]				1966[b]		
	Standard regions		Sub-regions	Counties	Standard regions[c]	Sub-regions	Counties
	Old	New					
Sources for							
England and Wales	1	2[d]	–	1[e]	3	–[f]	4[g]
Scotland	5	2[d]	5[h]	–	3 & 6	6[i]	–
Northern Ireland	–	–	–	–	7	7[i]	–

KEY: 1 = *Census 1961. England and Wales. Migration Tables*, London HMSO, 1966, tables 5 and 7.
2 = *Census 1961.* (special tabulations – unpublished).
3 = *Sample Census 1966. England and Wales. Migration Summary Tables*, Pt. I, London, HMSO, 1968, table 2.
4 = *Sample Census 1966. England and Wales. Migration Regional Reports*, London, HMSO, 1968, table 7.
5 = *Census 1961. Scotland.* vol. 8, *Internal Migration*, Edinburgh, HMSO, 1966, tables 5 and 17.
6 = *Sample Census 1966. Scotland. Migration Tables*, Pt. I, Edinburgh, HMSO, 1968–9, table 3.
7 = *Census of Population 1966. Northern Ireland. General Report*, Belfast, HMSO, 1968, table 11.

One-year data: five-year data not available.

One-year data and five-year data.

New standard regions only.

Within England and Wales only, plus immigrants from Scotland.

List of origins and destinations is shorter than in 1966, and breakdown is by sex only, not by age.

Some five-year data for males aged 15–64 is available from *Sample Census 1966* (special tabulations – unpublished).

Not broken down by age or by sex.

Within Scotland only. Subregions are slightly different from 1966, and breakdown is by sex only.

Within Scotland and Northern Ireland only.

The three sets of cross-section data from the Census form the most complete set of data in existence for Great Britain, but there are still limitations. The full matrix for Great Britain is available for 1961–6 and 1965–6, but the Scottish column in the 1960–1 matrix is not split by origin for the new standard English regions (the same problem applies to Northern Ireland for both years); also the Irish Republic Census of 1966 did not ask a migration question. Clearly, the first step in improving census data on migration would be to get the four census offices to co-operate more fully in the collection and processing of data, in order to provide comparable information on movements within the British Isles.

Another limitation is the lack of data on emigrants from all regions. This problem is inherent in the nature of a Census, and the only means of filling the gap is to use

[1] E.J. Thompson, 'Published data on interregional migration', *Greater London Research*, no. 2, June 1968, pp. 12–14.

material from other sources. Two possibilities are the International Passenger Survey[1] and the immigration figures of the main recipient countries (the United States, Canada, Australia, New Zealand and Western Europe). But even if these data were available by British standard regions, there still problems. Two other sources, must be considered less valuable: the Department of Employment's estimates of employee migration based on insurance cards were abandoned because the figures seriously exaggerated interregion movement (by a factor greater than two),[2] although the Department's new earnings survey could provide the information on mobility of employees that is at present unavai able;[3] the General Register Office's estimates of net migration based on information from electoral rolls, dwelling lists and National Health Service cards are 'tentative'.[4] Finally, two sample surveys provide interesting descriptive material on the pattern of and reasons for migration.[5]

Although the Census provides the best set of data available, it would be naive to suppose there are not associated methodological problems. In fact there are two:

(a) interpretation of the five-year migration data and their relationship to the one-year data,

(b) sampling problems.

We will consider these separately.

In the Census a migrant is defined as a person with different addresses at two separate points in time. The information is gathered by direct inquiry at a later date. The differences between five-year and one-year data arise from the length of the intervening period and there are two questions at issue. First, what do the five-year data mean? In particular, can it be assumed that one-year migrants are 'short-run' migrants and that five-year migrants are 'long-run'. Secondly, can the five year data be converted to an annual rate for purposes of comparison with the one-year data?

The notes to the *Migration Summary Tables* issue a warning:

The Census identifies one-year and five-year migrants. Some people are in both categories and appear in both the one-year and the five-year tables (most one-year migrants are five-year migrants too). It should be noted that this concept of migration fails to take into account the fact that some people have moved several times during the year before census or in the five years before census. Moreover the count of one-year migrants, by definition, excludes children under one year of age, and that of five-year migrants excludes children under five years of age .

[1] For a description of this survey, and a discussion of its accuracy see General Register Office, *Registrar General's Statistical Review of England and Wales for 1966*, Pt. III: *Commentary*, London, HMSO, 1970, pp. 10–19.

[2] *Ministry of Labour Gazette*, February 1968, p. 120. For details consult A.J. Brown, 'Surveys in Applied Economics: regional economics with special reference to the United Kingdom', *Economic Journal*, vol. 79, December 1969, p. 772 and H. Lind, 'Migration in Britain', NIESR research paper (unpublished), section 2 and appendix A.

[3] See A.R. Thatcher, 'The DEP's new earnings survey', *Statistical News*, no. 8, February 1970, pp. 11–13.

[4] See Thompson, 'Published data on interregional migration', p. 14.

[5] Government Social Survey, *Labour Mobility in Great Britain, 1953–63*, by A.I. Harris and R. Clausen, London, 1966 and *The Housing Survey in England and Wales, 1964*, by M. Woolf, London, 1967.

[6] General Register Office, *Sample Census 1966. England and Wales. Migration Summary Tables* (Pts I and II), London, HMSO, 1968, 'Notes', p. viii.

Table 3. *Different types of migrant*

	Region of residence	Migration pattern			Appearance in the data
		5 years ago	1 year ago	Now	
Stayer	A				Not in either 1-year or 5-year
	B	———————————————			data
	C				
'Ideal'	A				Migrant from A to B in both
migrant	B	———————		———	1-year and 5-year data
	C				
Typical	A				Migrant from A to B in 5-year
migrant	B	———	———————		data; not in 1-year data
	C				
Traveller	A				Migrant from A to C in 5-year
	B	———			data; migrant from B to C in
	C			———	1-year data
Returner	A			———	Not in 5-year data; migrant
	B	———	———		from B to A in 1-year data
	C				

The main logical possibilities are illustrated in table 3. The two problems mentioned in the quotation, of migrants who move from A to B to C within the period, and of the exclusion of children under five may be ignored, after noting that they are more acute for five-year than for one-year data. Table 3 shows, however, that there are at least four different types of migrant that might appear in either or both sets of data. The comment 'most one-year migrants are five-year migrants too' is correct, because two of the three groups that constitute the one-year migrants are also five-year migrants, but the direction of movement may differ between the two sets of data. There are two main types of 'distortion' — some migrants appear in one set of data but not in the other, which distorts the migration level, and some migrants move to the same destination from different origins, which distorts the direction. Therefore any attempt to convert the five-year data to annual rates by dividing by five would be hamstrung by the double counting of some migrants.[1]

Do the five-year data measure 'long-run' migration? In a country as small as Britain, distances are short, so that 'long-run' cannot refer to the journey time; it must therefore refer to the duration of residence, presumably at the destination. Again it is clear from consideration of table 3 that only 'typical' migrants, which are likely to be the most numerous, can be considered 'long-run' as having lived in region B for at least a year (which is hardly a very long period). So, if information on long-run migration is required, the solution is to inspect the birthplace tables, or (ideally) gather information directly on duration of residence.

Are the five-year data useful, then, even subject to all these problems? Their value lies in the fact that they summarise directly the net changes due to all types of migration over a five-year interval. This is of great value in regional population projections, if one is

---

[1] See also the notes to the census volumes.

predicting population distributions at five-year intervals. But for information on the dynamics of migration the one-year data are essential.

Each set of data on migration was gathered from a 10 per cent sample of the total population. This gives rise to problems both of bias and of sampling errors.

The appropriate sampling frame for migration is a register of persons at the end of the period of interest, from which a sample of persons may be selected and questioned. It is generally recognised that there are two main sources of bias. First, the sampling frame is a list of addresses and although efforts are made to keep it up to date they are inevitably unsuccessful, thus new addresses exist but are unknown, and others included in the list have disappeared. Secondly, the sample will be under-enumerated if not all the sample addresses are covered. These twin sources of deficiency are probably most serious for Greater London.

Further, whether or not bias exists, all estimates from a 10 per cent sample are subject to sampling error. A rough rule of thumb for estimating the size of the error is given in the notes to the census volumes. The special problem with migration is that migrants move in groups (families) rather than singly, so that there is a problem of clustering. In general this has the effect of increasing the standard of error of the estimate of total migration. The second volume of the *Migration Summary Tables* gives information on migration by family and by household.[1]

[1] General Register Office, *Sample Census 1966. England and Wales.*

CHAPTER TWO

MIGRATION MODELS

The theory of migration models is discussed in this section. There are two broad types, aggregate and individualistic, but the latter, in which the 'distance function' is fitted to data on individual moves from one geographical area, is ignored.[1] The aim of an aggregate migration model is to describe or explain the characteristics of the data on aggregate flows of migrants between geographical areas (summarised in one or several migration-flow matrices). There is considerable variety in the models suggested in the literature,[2] but most may be allocated to one of three main groups.

THE CURRENT STATE OF RESEARCH

Most work on migration has been done from the demographic rather than the economic viewpoint, with the primary aim of forecasting regional populations. Forecasts are made of net interregional and international migration, to supplement the basic demographic model of births and deaths using age and sex-specific survival and fertility rates.[3] In the last 30 years a large number of studies of interregional migration have been published, many of which use, explicitly or implicitly, a statistical model of migration-flows. With certain ambitious exceptions,[4] they fall into three main groups, *ad hoc* models, gravity models (both groups estimated by regression or analysis of covariance methods) and Markov chain models.

The *ad hoc* models regress net (or gross) migration-flows (or rates) on a set of independent variables selected as possible determinants of migration. For example Oliver

---

[1] See T. Hägerstrand, 'Migration and area. A survey of a sample of Swedish migration fields and hypothetical considerations of their genesis' in *Migration in Sweden: a symposium*, Lund, Sweden, Royal University of Lund, Department of Geography, 1957, for a discussion of this type of model.

[2] See R.L. Morrill, *Migration and the Spread and Growth of Urban Settlement*, Lund, Sweden, Royal University of Lund, Department of Geography, 1965.

[3] A summary of the literature on population and migration analysis, and a large (but incomplete) bibliography can be found in J. Willis, 'Population Growth and Movement', Centre for Environmental Studies working paper (unpublished). Detailed accounts of the algebra of demographic projection models are given in N. Keyfitz 'Matrix multiplication as a technique of population analysis', *Milbank Memorial Fund Quarterly*, vol. 42, October 1964, and *Introduction to the Mathematics of Population*, Reading (Mass.), Addison-Wesley, 1968; A. Rogers, *Matrix Analysis of Interregional Growth and Distribution*, Berkeley (Cal.), University of California Press, 1968.

[4] For example the grand schemes in D.O. Price, 'A mathematical model of migration suitable for simulation on an electronic computer', *Proceedings, International Population Conference (Vienna) 1959*, pp. 665–73 and R. McGinnis, G.C. Myers and J. Pilger, 'Internal migration as a stochastic process', *Proceedings, 34th Session, International Statistical Institute (Ottawa) 1963*, vol. 40, book 1, p. 446.

and Corry both use analysis of covariance,[1] testing not only for regional differences in intercepts but also for differences in slopes for the model:

$$\frac{N_{it}}{P_{it}} = A_i + B_i X_{it} + V_{it} ,\tag{1}$$

where N = net or gross (in or out) migration-flow (of insurance card holders),

P = total population (total insured persons),

X = unemployment percentage,

i = refers to the ith region,

t = refers to the tth time period,

and V is an additive error term.

The gravity models work at a different level of aggregation and use a log-linear not a linear form. Several specifications, all of which could be called gravitational, are available in the literature. A simple version is

$$M_{ij} = A \left(\frac{P_i P_j}{D_{ij}}\right)^{B_1} \cdot \frac{X_i^{B_2}}{X_j^{B_3}} \cdot V_{ij} ,\tag{2}$$

where M_{ij} = migration from the ith to the jth region,

P_i = population of the ith region (P_i and P_j represent the 'masses' at i and j),

D_{ij} = distance between region i and region j,

X_i = the value of an explanatory variable X for region i, taken to be relevant to its attractiveness or unattractiveness,

X_j = the value of X for region j,

and V_{ij} is a multiplicative error term.

This model is easily generalised to include more explanatory variables, or regional dummies may be used to estimate 'push' and 'pull' factors peculiar to particular regions.[2]

The simplest Markov chain model takes the migration flow matrix $\mathbf{M_3}$, with diagonal elements equal to intra-regional migrants plus non-migrants,[3] and, rather like input—output analysis, assumes that the transition proportions, $q_{ij} = M_{ij}/P_i$ are stable, that is constant or changing in a predictable way over time.

The full matrix of transition proportions, $\mathbf{Q}$, may then be used to transform an initial vector of regional populations at the start of the period into a population vector at the end of the period. This type of model generates forecasts of future populations in conjunction with models of births, deaths, and interregional migration, but the predictive power of the projection depends entirely on the validity of the initial assumption

[1] F.R. Oliver, 'Interregional migration and unemployment, 1951–61', *Journal of the Royal Statistical Society* (series A), vol. 127, 1964, pp. 42–75; B.A. Corry, 'Interregional mobility and unemployment. The U.K. experience 1952–62' (unpublished).

[2] A discussion of early gravity models is to be found in W. Isard (ed.) *Methods of Regional Analysis: an approach to regional science*, Cambridge (Mass.), MIT Press, 1960 and H. Ter Heide, 'Migration models and their significance for population forecasts', *Milbank Memorial Fund Quarterly*, vol. 41, June 1963, pp. 56–76. More recent work is summarised in Rogers, *Matrix Analysis of Interregional Growth and Distribution*.

[3] Instead of $\mathbf{M_1}$ (with zero diagonal elements) the matrix normally used in regression studies (see table 1).

at q_{ij} is constant. The main applied studies are Rogers on interregional movement,[1] and Blumen, Kogan and McCarthy on inter-industrial movement.[2] The latter introduces a generalisation known as the mover—stayer model.

An interesting feature of migration studies is that nearly all the models fall into one of the three groups listed above, but rarely does a study attempt to use models from more than one group. This is partly because most authors conceive the basic problem of discovering the determinants of migration-flows) rather narrowly as the problem of obtaining an adequate specification in terms of conventional criteria such as R^2, and partly because the data available determine the nature of the dependent variable and therefore the model used. But a more important reason is that the different types of model offer conflicting hypotheses about the behaviour of migration-flows at the various levels of aggregation. So which is the best model? This question is discussed below, but it is interesting to note at this stage that even the relatively few authors who use two types of model, for example, Rogers[3] and Predetti,[4] generally ignore the conflict between them. An exception is the article by Kelley and Weiss,[5] but even here the conclusion that a net flow model is superior to a very crude Markov chain model is reached by rather strange reasoning.

AD HOC MODELS

The title *ad hoc* is used in this paper to identify a group of models which attempt to discover whether net migration is associated with various economic (or other) explanatory factors. On the basis of elementary economic reasoning,[6] net migration into a region may be expected to be a function of the regional wage rate or unemployment rate, or regional income *per capita*. Researchers attempt to realise this expectation by specifying a linear regression model. In the case of a cross-section study,[7] the model might take the form

$$\frac{N_i}{P_i} = A + BX_i + V_i , \qquad (3)$$

[1] *Matrix Analysis of Interregional Growth and Distribution.*

[2] I. Blumen, M. Kogan and P.J. McCarthy, *The Industrial Mobility of Labor as a Probability Process,* Ithaca, Cornell University Press, 1955.

[3] *Matrix Analysis of Interregional Growth and Distribution.*

[4] A. Predetti, *Le Componenti Economiche, Sociale e Demografiche della Mobilita Interna della Popolazione Italiana*, Milan, Vita e Pensiero (Scotti), 1965.

[5] A.C. Kelley and L.W. Weiss, 'Markov processes and economic analysis: the case of migration', *Econometrica*, vol. 37, April 1969, pp. 280–97.

[6] Ibid. p. 283 for example.

[7] Some examples are C. Blanco, 'The determinants of inter-State population movements', *Journal of Regional Science*, vol. 5, no. 1, 1963, pp. 77–84; B. Okun, 'Interstate population migration and state income inequality: a simultaneous equation approach', *Economic Development and Cultural Change*, vol. 16, no. 2, part 1, January 1968, pp. 297–313. Other references can be found in Willis, 'Population Growth and Movement', pp. 57–61.

where N_i/P_i = the net migration rate,

$\quad\quad X_i$ is the explanatory variable,

$\quad\quad V_i$ is a stochastic term,

and i denotes the ith region.

Results are satisfactory, but not striking, in terms of the conventional criteria of a good R^2 and significant coefficients with the correct signs.

Many of the problems associated with cross-section *ad hoc* models also affect cross-section gravity models, in particular the wide variety of explanatory variables nominated by researchers. The discussion in the next section is therefore also relevant to *ad hoc* models. But there are two papers using time-series data for Great Britain which deserve special consideration, because they illustrate the theoretical problems associated with *ad hoc* models.[1]

Oliver uses three specifications.[2] The first is of the form

$$\frac{N_{it}}{P_{it}} = A_i + B_i X_{it} + V_{it} ,\tag{4}$$

already mentioned. The second includes the national unemployment rate $\bar{X}_t$, as an explanatory variable:

$$\frac{N_{it}}{P_{it}} = A_i + B_i X_{it} + C_i \bar{X}_t + V_{it} .\tag{5}$$

The third specification

$$\frac{N_{it}}{P_{it}} = A_i + D_i(X_{it} - \bar{X}_t) + V_{it} ,\tag{6}$$

merely tests the parameter restriction $B_i = -C_i$.

These models are fitted to 90 time-series observations (nine regions by ten years), and in estimation all the logical possibilities are explored. Oliver fits the following equations:

(i) A regression of N_{it}/P_{it} on X_{it} and $\bar{X}_t$, assuming $A_i = A$, $B_i = B$ and $C_i = C$ (for (5) – one equation, 90 observations, three parameters).

(ii) A regression assuming differences in intercepts, that is allowing A_i to differ, but with $B_i = B$ and $C_i = C$ (for (5) – one equation, 90 observations, 11 parameters).

(iii) Separate regressions assuming differences in intercepts and in slopes, that is allowing A_i, B_i and C_i to differ between regions (for (5) – nine equations, each with ten observations, each with three parameters).

In addition Oliver estimates an analysis of variance model

$$\frac{N_{it}}{P_{it}} = A + B_i Q_{it} ,\tag{7}$$

[1] Oliver, 'Interregional migration and unemployment, 1951–61'; A.B. Jack, 'A short-run model of interregional migration', *Manchester School*, vol. 38, no. 1, March 1970. The Scottish Council report, *Emigration and Immigration: the Scottish situation*, Edinburgh, 1966, also uses the same data (produced by the Department of Employment) which, as noted on p. 48 above, is subject to severe errors.

[2] 'Interregional migration and unemployment, 1951–61'.

here the Q_{it} are regional dummies (zero except for the ith region, where Q_{it} takes the value one for all time periods).

A.B. Jack shows that a migration model at the net or gross flow level may be built up from a model of M_{ij} using the basic identities of internal migration outlined on pages 4–5.[1] Since it is proposed to use a development of this approach in this paper it will be useful to follow the implications of his assumptions.

Unfortunately his total immigration (I_i) and total emigration (E_i) are derived from separate equations for I_{ij} (the number of immigrants from region j to region i) and E_{ij} the number of emigrants to region j from region i) although $I_{ij} = E_{ij}$.[2] The emigration equation[3] is

$$\frac{M_{ijt}}{P_{it}} = a_{ij} + a_1 \frac{P_{jt}}{P_{it}} f(X_{jt}) + a_2 \frac{X_{it}}{P_{it}}, \tag{8}$$

where M_{ijt} = migration of insured male employees from region i to region j during t,

$\quad a_{ij}$ = the 'long-run' emigration from i to j,

$\quad P_{it}$ = the number of insured males in region i,

$\quad f(X_{jt})$ is a function of the unemployment rates experienced by region j,

$\quad X_{it}$ = the average unemployment rate in region i during t,

and a_{ij} = the 'long-term rate of annual emigration' from i to j.

But the following equation is for immigration to the jth region from region i:[4]

$$\frac{M_{ijt}}{P_{jt}} = b_{ij} + b_1 \frac{P_{it}}{P_{jt}} f(X_{jt}) + b_2 \frac{X_{it}}{P_{jt}}, \tag{9}$$

where b_{ij} is the 'long-run' immigration to j from i.

Multiplying (9) through by P_{jt}/P_{it} gives

$$\frac{M_{ijt}}{P_{it}} = b_{ij} \frac{P_{jt}}{P_{it}} + b_1 f(X_{jt}) + b_2 \frac{X_{it}}{P_{it}}, \tag{10}$$

so that, from (8) and (10),

$$a_{ij} = b_{ij} \frac{P_{jt}}{P_{it}}, \quad a_1 \frac{P_{jt}}{P_{it}} = b_1 \quad \text{and} \quad a_2 = b_2. \tag{11}$$

Jack sums equation (8) over j to form a set of emigration equations for E_i, to estimate a_1 and a_2 for each region, and equation (9) over i to form a set of immigration equations for I_i, to estimate b_1 and b_2 for each region. Therefore he assumes that a_1 and a_2 are constant over j, and b_1 and b_2 are constant over i, which implies that $a_2 (= b_2)$ is constant over i and over j. In fact the estimates for a_2 range from 0·033 to 0·103,[5] and

[1] 'A short-run model of interregional migration'.

[2] This approach is admitted to be faulty, but retained in a later paper '… the only way in which emigration equations could be estimated was by a simplifying mis-specification which is bound to have affected the emigration results'. (A.B. Jack, 'Interregional migration in Great Britain: some cross-sectional evidence', *Scottish Journal of Political Economy*, vol. 18, June 1971, p. 159).

[3] 'A short-run model of interregional migration', p. 18, eqn. (3).

[4] Ibid. p. 19, eqn. (6).

[5] Ibid. p. 23, table I – a seventh of the estimated coefficients for Wales (0·232) and London (0·718).

for b_2 from $0 \cdot 025$ to $0 \cdot 179$.[1] But the constraints on a_1 and b_1 are more complicated; a_1 is assumed constant over j, but may differ over i and so represent the set of parameters a_{1i}, and b_1 is assumed constant over i, but may differ over j and so represent the set b_{1j}. Therefore, from (11), $a_{1i}/b_{1j} = P_{it}/P_{jt}$. This specifies that the ratio of two constants is equal to the ratio of two variables, an unlikely but possible restriction (if regional populations remain in fixed proportions to one another over time). So the restrictions implicit in the model are ignored, because a_1 and a_2 are estimated by one set of emigration equations and b_1 and b_2 by another set of immigration equations.

Although Jack fails to take into account the restrictions on parameters implied by his assumptions, he does provide a glimpse of a possible approach to developing net migration models, by first specifying a model of M_{ij}, linear in terms of rates of flows, then summing over i or j to get immigrants and emigrants, and taking the difference of immigrants and emigrants to get an equation for net migration. Consider for example the simple linear cross-section model

$$\frac{M_{ij}}{P_i P_j} = A_{ij} + B_1 X_i + B_2 X_j . \tag{12}$$

The gross and net rate equations for migration from region i are:

$$\frac{I_i}{P_i} = \frac{\Sigma_j M_{ji}}{P_i} = \Sigma_j A_{ji} P_j + B_1 \Sigma_j X_j P_j + B_2 X_i \Sigma_j P_j , \tag{13}$$

$$\frac{E_i}{P_i} = \frac{\Sigma_j M_{ij}}{P_i} = \Sigma_j A_{ij} P_j + B_1 X_i \Sigma_j P_j + B_2 \Sigma_j X_j P_j , \tag{14}$$

$$\frac{N_i}{P_i} = \frac{I_i - E_i}{P_i} = \Sigma_j (A_{ji} - A_{ij}) P_j + (B_2 - B_1)[X_i \Sigma_j P_j - \Sigma_j X_j P_j] , \tag{15}$$

noting that all summations over j exclude $j = i$.
Adding and subtracting $X_i P_i$ within the last bracket of (15) gives the net migration rate equation:

$$\frac{N_i}{P_i} = \Sigma_j (A_{ji} - A_{ij}) P_j + (B_2 - B_1)[X_i - \bar{X}] \bar{P} , \tag{16}$$

where $\bar{P} = \Sigma_j P_j$ (the total population) and $\bar{X} = \Sigma_j X_j P_j / \Sigma_j P_j$ (the weighted mean of variable X), and for both $\bar{P}$ and $\bar{X}$ the summation over j *includes* $j = i$.

For estimation purposes, assuming that cross-section data are available, an additional hypothesis about the behaviour of A_{ij} is required. The simplest assumption is that $A_{ji} = A_{ij}$. For example, A_{ij} may take the gravitational form $A_{ij} = A_0 + A_1 D_{ij}$. From equation (12) the net balance of migrants is $(M_{ji} - M_{ij})/P_i P_j = (B_2 - B_1)(X_i - X_j)$, and summation over j gives the net migration rate:

$$\frac{N_i}{P_i} = (B_2 - B_1)(X_i - \bar{X}) \bar{P} . \tag{17}$$

The net migration rate in this model is a proportional function of the difference between the regional and the national value of X_i.

[1] Ibid. p. 24, table II.

The linear model displays great flexibility, since it may be estimated at different levels of aggregation, depending on the data available. In general the more disaggregated the data, the more information may be derived on the values of coefficients. At the net rate or net balance level, the value of $B_2 - B_1$ can be estimated, at the gross rate level B_1 and B_2 can be estimated separately, and at the M_{ij} level the values of A_0, A_1, B_1, B_2 can all be estimated separately. If time-series data are available, then the assumption $A_{ij} = A_{ji}$ is not necessary for estimation purposes. But if the assumption is felt to be a reasonable description of reality, it may be used to eliminate the constant term in the net rate equation. Otherwise the only modification (which may or may not be justifiable from an economic point of view) is to allow B_1 to differ by region of destination (B_{1j}) and B_2 by region of origin (B_{2i}) which gives gross rate equations for M_{ijt}:

$$\frac{I_{it}}{P_{it}} = \Sigma_j A_{ji} P_{jt} + B_{1i} \Sigma_j X_{jt} P_{jt} + X_{it} \Sigma_j B_{2j} P_{jt} \tag{18}$$

and
$$\frac{E_{it}}{P_{it}} = \Sigma_j A_{ij} P_{jt} + X_{it} \Sigma_j B_{1j} P_{jt} + B_{2i} \Sigma_j X_{jt} P_{jt} ; \tag{19}$$

also the net rate equation:

$$\frac{N_{it}}{P_{it}} = \Sigma_j (A_{ji} - A_{ij}) P_{jt} + (B_{1i} - B_{2i}) \Sigma_j X_{jt} P_{jt} + (B_2{}^* - B_1{}^*) X_{it} , \tag{20}$$

where $B_1{}^* = \Sigma_j B_{1j} P_{jt}$ and $B_2{}^* = \Sigma_j B_{2j} P_{jt}$.

Equations (18) and (19) have clear implications for Jack's work. If Jack had used one basic equation for M_{ijt}, say (8), and allowed a_1 and a_2 to differ by region of origin and of destination respectively (a_{1i} and a_{2j}), he would have been justified in estimating separate emigration and immigration equations, although (18) and (19) also impose complicated constraints on the values of B_{1j} and B_{2i} which should be taken into account.

One further problem is the choice of an appropriate stochastic term. Suppose that a stochastic term, V_{ij}, is added to (12) and is normally distributed with zero mean. The stochastic term of the net rate equation (17) is $V_i{}^*$, where $V_i{}^* = \Sigma_j P_j (V_{ji} - V_{ij})$ and clearly $V_i{}^*$ is normally distributed with zero mean. The problem is to make an appropriate assumption about the variance of V_{ij}. The most reasonable assumption is that V_{ij} has variance $S^2/P_i^2 P_j^2$, where S^2 is an unknown constant.[1] In this case $V_i{}^*$ has variance $2(n-1)S^2/P_i^2$ and, in order to estimate (12) or (17) by ordinary least squares, one merely has to multiply (12) throughout by $P_i P_j$ and (17) throughout by P_i, in effect fitting the model to M_{ij} or N_i rather than to $M_{ij}/P_i P_j$ or N_i/P_i.

The implications of linear migration models could be explored further, but one important conclusion may be stated. If a net migration model is to be estimated (by choice or because of data limitations) then it should be derived explicitly from a M_{ij} model. Net migration models have remained far too long in the realms of theoretical 'ad hoc-ery'.

---

[1] This uses conventional assumptions, but if the variance of $V_i{}^*$ is felt to be too large the appropriate adjustment is to assume that there is negative autocorrelation between certain V_{ij}.

This section examines a set of models based on an analogy with physical phenomena. Briefly, if the population of a region is considered as a mass concentrated at its centre, then migration between a pair of regions is a function of the 'gravitational attraction' of the two regions:

$$M_{ij} = f_1(P_i, P_j, D_{ij}).$$ (21)

But because there are differences between regions (not only economic), the migration function contains 'push' and 'pull' factors — the 'push' factors tending to increase or decrease the level of migration out of the region, and the 'pull' factors to increase or decrease the level of migration into the region:

$$M_{ij} = f_2(P_i, P_j, D_{ij}, X_i, X_j).$$ (22)

The difference between (22) and the models of the last section, for example (12), is that (22) is normally specified as a log-linear function and this function is directly estimated on census cross-section data for M_{ij}.

It is not clear who first applied gravity models to migration. The usual nomination is Ravenstein who expressed his *a priori* expectations in the form of 'laws' as early as 1889.[1] The two earliest pieces of work related directly to modern theory are by Makower Marschak, and Robinson[2] and Zipf.[3] The former fitted the model

$$M_{ij} = A \frac{P_i P_j}{D_{ij}{}^B} \cdot \frac{(X_i - X_j)}{X_j},$$ (23)

where X_i is the percentage unemployed in county i, to data on in-migrants to Oxfordshire from all other counties in the 15 years before 1936. For males and females together R^2 is $0{\cdot}80$[4] and the estimate of B is significantly different from zero. Zipf relates a measure of interaction I_{ij} (equal to $M_{ij} + M_{ji}$ in the case of migration) to $P_i P_j / D_{ij}$, using implicitly the functional form

$$I_{ij} = A \left(\frac{P_i P_j}{D_{ij}}\right)^B,$$ (24)

since he plots 'interaction phenomena', which include railway journeys and telephone calls as well as human migrants,[5] against the factor $P_i P_j / D_{ij}$ on log–log paper and searches for straight lines.

---

[1] E.G. Ravenstein, 'The laws of migration', *Journal of the Royal Statistical Society*, vol. 38, 1885 and vol. 42, 1889.

[2] H. Makower, J. Marschak and H.W. Robinson, 'Studies in mobility of labour', *Oxford Economic Papers*, no. 1, October 1938, pp. 83–123, no. 2, May 1939, pp. 70–97 and no. 4, September 1940, pp. 39–62.

[3] G.K. Zipf, 'The $P_1 P_2 / D$ hypothesis on the inter-city movement of persons', *American Sociological Review*, vol. 11, October 1946, pp. 677–86.

[4] This in fact measures the fit of a linear function of $\log D_{ij}$ to $\log \{(M_{ij} X_j / [P_i P_j (X_i - X_j)]\}$.

[5] See Isard (ed.), *Methods of Regional Analysis*, pp. 503–4.

Nearly all gravity models use the log-linear form, although linear models are just as feasible. But consensus on the form of the specification is matched by wide differences between authors on the exact way in which the dependent and independent variables (gravity and explanatory) should enter the equation, and which explanatory variables should be used.

Practically all recent research has used M_{ij} (or $M_{ij}/P_i P_j$) as the dependent variable, but because of Zipf's use of 'total interaction' without regard to direction (despite one's interest in direction rather than size), Somermeijer has specified a model which embodies $M_{ij} + M_{ji} = AP_i P_j/D_{ij}{}^B$ as a constraint.[1] The model is:

$$M_{ij} = \frac{P_i P_j}{2D_{ij}{}^B}[A_1 + A_2(X_i - X_j)], \tag{25}$$

where X_i is an economic variable associated with the ith region. Clearly,

$$M_{ij} + M_{ji} = A_1\frac{P_i P_j}{D_{ij}{}^B} \text{ and } M_{ij} - M_{ji} = A_2\frac{P_i P_j}{D_{ij}{}^B}(X_i - X_j). \tag{26}$$

On the face of it the specification is plausible and could be generalised. For example, $(P_i P_j/D_{ij})^B$ or $(X_i - X_j)^C$ might be used,[2] although certain other specifications, like $A_2 X_i/X_j$ do not imply the Zipf model. But there are problems of estimation: one method would be to estimate the two equations (26) jointly by ordinary least squares,[3] but this is only possible if $M_{ij} - M_{ji}$ and $X_i - X_j$ are of the same sign throughout,[4] which is quite a stringent condition. Ter Heide reports that Somermeijer used an iterative method of estimation.[5]

The real criticism of this model is that there is no obvious reason to embody the constraint on 'total interaction', and that by using a mixed multiplicative-additive model of migration the specification of the explanatory part of the model is restricted to certain forms and the estimation made unnecessarily complex. It is far easier to stick to linear forms as in the last section or to log-linear forms as in the rest of this section.

Nearly all the logically possible alternatives have been used for the gravitational part of the model at one time or other. The most common forms are:

$$M_{ij} = A\frac{P_i P_j}{D_{ij}{}^B} \text{ (other variables)} \tag{27}$$

[1] W.H. Somermeijer, 'Een analyse van de binnenlandse migratie in Nederland tot 1947 en van 1948–1957', *Statistische en Econometrische Onderzoekingen*, 3rd quarter 1961, pp. 115–74 (discussed in English in Ter Heide, 'Migration models and their significance for population forecasts').

[2] As long as C is an odd integer, positive or negative.

[3] This can be done by regressing jointly $\log[(M_{ij} + M_{ji})/P_i P_j]$ and $\log[(M_{ij} - M_{ji})/P_i P_j(X_i - X_j)]$ on $\log D_{ij}$, constraining the slope parameter to the same value but assuming different intercepts. The assumption is that $M_{ij} + M_{ji} = A_1 \cdot V_{ij} \cdot P_i P_j/D_{ij}{}^B$ and $M_{ij} - M_{ji} = A_2(X_i - X_j)W_{ij}P_i P_j/D_{ij}{}^B$, where V_{ij} and W_{ij} are stochastic variables such that $\log V_{ij}$ and $\log W_{ij}$ are normally distributed with zero means and constant variances. Using this method of estimation, the Somermeijer model complete with stochastic terms is
$$M_{ij} = [A_1 V_{ij} + A_2(X_i - X_j)W_{ij}]P_i P_j/2D_{ij}{}^B.$$

[4] Otherwise the logarithm of a negative number is required.

[5] 'Migration models and their significance for population forecasts'.

and $M_{ij} = A \left(\dfrac{P_i P_j}{D_{ij}}\right)^B$ (other variables). (28)

The form

$$\frac{M_{ij}}{P_i} = A \left(\frac{P_j}{D_{ij}}\right)^B \quad \text{(other variables)} \tag{29}$$

has also been used. Some of the earlier workers were willing to assume *a priori* that the distance parameter might take the value $\frac{1}{2}$, 1, or 2, but most studies estimate the parameter B and the other parameters of the model without inserting *a priori* values. The use of arbitrary fixed weights W_1 and W_2 to form terms like $W_1 P_i W_2 P_j / D_{ij}{}^B$ merely shifts the value of the constant term.[1]

The gravity model is log-linear, so that explanatory variables normally enter the model as follows:

$$M_{ij} = A \left(\frac{P_i P_j}{D_{ij}}\right)^{B_1} \cdot \frac{X_i{}^{B_2}}{X_j{}^{B_3}} . \tag{30}$$

But sometimes the form $(X_i / X_j)^{B_4}$ is used. The parameter B_4 embodies the constraint $B_2 = -B_3$, which saves one degree of freedom. The Makower, Marschak, Robinson form, $(X_i - X_j)/X_j$, has fallen out of fashion. Despite the differences in equation form, everyone agrees basically that regional differences in 'push' and 'pull' may exist. The existence of 'pull' (factors that attract migrants to some regions rather than others) is a reasonable hypothesis, but 'push' (factors that move migrants away from certain regions) is less acceptable; Lowry for one tends to imply that regional differentials in 'push' are unimportant and that people are likely to migrate when they reach certain points in their life cycle.[2] In this case regional differences in emigration rates will merely be due to differences in the composition of the regional populations. But from an empirical point of view the existence of 'push' or 'pull' (or both) can be tested as long as one can specify what factors (economic or otherwise) may be expected to affect interregional migration.

The striking thing about migration studies is the variety of explanatory variables that have been tried. The list includes (as a sample):

Economic factors: unemployment rates, growth of employment, activity rates, wage rates, wage earnings, income *per capita*, cost of living differentials, prices of housing, retail sales levels, gas or electricity consumption.
Demographic factors: population densities, rates of natural increase, proportions in certain age groups.
Sociological factors: the proportion of the population of a certain type (professional, farmers, students, in growing industries, in armed forces, in urban areas).
Physical factors: mean weekly sunshine, mean rainfall, mean temperature; also, it is often suggested that distance should be measured in social or economic terms.

All of these can, in particular cases and combinations, claim some plausibility as factors tending to increase or inhibit movement from the origin or towards the destination

[1] Ibid; see also Isard, *Methods of Regional Analysis*.

[2] I.S. Lowry, *Migration and Metropolitan Growth: two analytical models*, Los Angeles, University of California Press, 1966.

which they apply, but most of them can be applied injudiciously, and some combinations of them may introduce multicollinearity.

Some authors, for example Sahota,[1] use regional dummies in gravity models together with explanatory variables in order to pick up effects not identified by other variables. It is not generally realised that a full analysis of covariance approach is a viable (and logically prior) alternative to an explanatory gravity (or linear) model, since it may be used to test for the existence of regional differences in 'push' and 'pull'. There is no sense in estimating an explanatory model if the null hypothesis of no difference in 'push' and 'pull' between regions is accepted. If the explanatory variables turn out insignificant in an estimated regression model, as experienced by Lowry,[2] then one has to fall back on the covariance model anyway.

Suppose the analysis of covariance model is log-linear as follows:

$$\log M_{ij} = A + B \log(P_i P_j / D_{ij}) + \Sigma_i C_{1i} \log QI_i + \Sigma_j C_{2j} \log QJ_j , \qquad (31)$$

where QI_i is a 'push' dummy variable, with $\log QI_i$ taking the value one when migration is out of the ith region and zero otherwise, and QJ_j is a 'pull' dummy variable, with $\log QJ_j$ taking the value one when migration is into the jth region and zero otherwise.

To avoid definitional multicollinearity, one each of the QI_i and the QJ_i dummies must be dropped when estimating the covariance model. The interpretation of the model is as follows: migration between regions may be predicted from a gravity model, but there exist unidentified regional differences which raise or lower the level of migration into or out of each region. The contribution of these unknown 'push' and 'pull' factors is summarised in the values of the coefficients of the 'push' and 'pull' dummies. One hopes that it is possible to identify the causes of the observed regional differences given knowledge of the estimated coefficients. The tests of hypotheses available in the covariance approach are outlined in chapter 4, where a linear covariance model is applied to subregional data.

The fundamental difference between *ad hoc* and gravity models is the assumption of linearity in the first case and log-linearity in the second. It is a curious historical accident that M_{ij} models have used log-linear functional forms, but net rate models have used linear forms. Both types of model are based on the assumption that migration is a turnover process, that for economic and sociological reasons people migrate at various stages of their life cycle, and therefore the so called 'push' and 'pull' factors act by distorting the basically equal exchange system of migration (predicted in the case of the log-linear model by the gravitational hypothesis) that would be observed in the absence of differences between regions.

MARKOV CHAIN MODELS

Suppose information is available for a given time period on the migration-flow matrix M_3 (with diagonal elements non-migrants plus intra-regional migrants). The sum of elements by rows is P_i, the population in region i at the start of the period, and the sum

[1] 'An economic analysis of internal migration in Brazil'.

[2] *Migration and Metropolitan Growth*; only one variable out of four, unemployment 'pull', turned out to be significant.

61

by columns is P_{i+1}, the regional population at the end of the period.

The basic assumption of Markov chain theory is that the coefficients $q_{ij} = M_{ij}/P_i$ of the transition matrix $\mathbf{Q}$ are stable, either constant or changing in a predictable way over time. Since only one cross-section of data is normally available, the usual assumption is that the coefficients are constant. From this simple assumption several important theorems may be derived,[1] but it should be noted immediately how restrictive it is. The level of migration out of each region is assumed to be a constant proportion over time of that region's population at the start of the period, and the emigrants are allocated to other regions in unvarying proportions. In terms of 'push' and 'pull', 'push' is a constant proportion of the population of origin, and the relative 'pulls' of other regions on a given region's migrants also remain constant (despite possible changes over time in the relative sizes of regional populations). The simple Markov chain model is therefore just a mechanical device, particularly suitable for making projections of regional populations, but denying the influence of any variable factors except population of the region of origin.

The simple Markov chain model is a very crude representation of the process of interregional migration. But there are ways in which it might be generalised or modified. The movers—stayers model is a simple generalisation suggested by Blumen, Kogan and McCarthy in their work on inter-industrial movement.[2] Regional populations are divided into two groups of persons, movers and stayers, and the movers move between regions according to a transition matrix $\mathbf{Q}^*$. Therefore the $\mathbf{Q}$ matrix defined above may be disaggregated into

$$\mathbf{Q} = \mathbf{S} + (\mathbf{I_n} - \mathbf{S})\mathbf{Q}^*, \tag{32}$$

where both $\mathbf{Q}$ and $\mathbf{Q}^*$ are transition matrices, and $\mathbf{S}$ and $(\mathbf{I_n} - \mathbf{S})$ are diagonal matrices.[3] For example, if 10 per cent of the population change residence each year, $\mathbf{S}$ will be a diagonal matrix with elements 0.9 and $(\mathbf{I_n} - \mathbf{S})$ a diagonal matrix with elements 0.1.

Unless the elements of $\mathbf{S}$ change over time the disaggregation is not very useful, because $\mathbf{Q}$ is constant if $\mathbf{S}$ and $\mathbf{Q}^*$ are both constant, and the usual theorems still hold for $\mathbf{Q}$. However, if $\mathbf{Q}^*$ is constant and $\mathbf{S}$ varies, then the elements of $\mathbf{Q}$ vary over time. The problem that Blumen, Kogan and McCarthy discuss in detail — who are the stayers? — is simply resolved in the case of interregional migration by assuming that all persons not reporting a change in residence are stayers, and therefore that $\mathbf{Q}^*$ applies to all migrants whether intra-regional or interregional. Clearly, assuming $\mathbf{Q}^*$ constant is more reasonable than assuming $\mathbf{Q}$ constant, because the level of migration is allowed to vary regionally, although the pattern of migration is still assumed to be rigidly tied to total migration from the region of origin.

The basic advantage of the Markov chain model is that it establishes a set of coefficients that may be multiplied into regional populations to form estimates of the level of interregional migration. But the method of forming the matrix of fixed coefficients, $\mathbf{Q}$, by dividing row elements by the row sum, is not the only approach. One could divide column elements by the column sum, but this matrix is even less plausible than the

---

[1] See J.G. Kemeny and J.L. Snell, *Finite Markov Chains*, Princeton (NJ), Van Nostrand, 1960, ch. 4 and Rogers, *Matrix Analysis of Interregional Growth and Distribution*.

[2] *The Industrial Mobility of Labor as a Probability Process*.

[3] All matrices are $n \times n$, where n is the number of regions.

Markov one. Two main alternatives suggest themselves, both taking into account the population at j as well as at i. Either

$$q'_{ij} = \frac{M_{ij}}{P_i P_j}, \tag{33}$$

which simply says that q'_{ij}, sometimes called the migration index,[1] is constant over time. However $\Sigma_j q'_{ij}$ is not equal to one as it is in the Markov chain model, so the q'_i cannot be interpreted as probabilities.[2] Or

$$q''_{ij} = \frac{M_{ij}}{P_i P_{j+1}}, \tag{34}$$

where P_{j+1} again signifies the post-migration population of j. This assumption says that the elements of the migration-flow matrix bear a constant relationship to the corresponding row and column sums. This sort of matrix (of probabilities, since $\Sigma_i \Sigma_j q''_{ij} = 1$) is to be found in information theory,[3] but it is even more restrictive (and unlikely) than the Markov chain assumption, because the elements of the row and column sum vectors are constrained to constant proportions. Anyway P_{j+1} is not known until the M_{ij} have been forecast.

Therefore (33) is the more plausible alternative to the Markov chain model (a mover–stayer version could be used). Forecasting by means of the coefficients q'_{ij} is straightforward and the pattern of migration (as well as the level of migration out of each region) adjusts to changing relative sizes of regional populations.

To summarise, if a mechanical forecasting device is required, the simple Markov chain model is not the only model available, nor is it the most plausible, even in its mover–stayer form, in terms of regression models discussed already. The set of coefficients q'_{ij} may be expected to produce better results, although all forecasting devices of this type are subject to the fundamental criticism that the coefficients may be expected to change over time.

THE RELATIONSHIP BETWEEN THE THREE MODELS

In this section an attempt is made to compare the types of model discussed above. The ad hoc model is the theoretical manifestation of the attempt to correlate the net migration rate and various independent variables. From a logical point of view it may be derived from a linear migration model (of M_{ij}), noting that the assumption $A_{ji} = A_{ij}$ eliminates the constant term.[4] The basic advantage of the linear model is that it may be estimated at all levels of aggregation, depending on the data available. In contrast the log-linear gravity model, which is normally estimated on cross-section data, may only be estimated (by normal methods) at the M_{ij} level of aggregation. Unlike the two regression

---

[1] The dependent variable of the linear regression model discussed on p. 56.

[2] If $q'_{ij} = q'_{ji}$ the pair of regions i and j exchange equal numbers of migrants.

[3] See, for example, H. Theil, *Economics and Information Theory*, Amsterdam, North-Holland, 1967.

[4] This assumption is normally essential in the case of cross-section models.

models, the Markov chain model is not fitted by a least squares criterion. The observed pattern of migration during one time period is summarised in a set of fixed coefficients and assumed to remain the same in the future. Only one variable factor is allowed to affect the level of migration – the size of the population of the region of origin; this is a highly restrictive assumption which fortunately is not the only alternative open to us.

Essentially there are two main groups of migration models, fixed-proportions models and regression models. The models available are summarised in table 4. In selecting a particular model, two questions must be answered: should a fixed-proportions or a regression model be used, and which member of the group selected should actually be applied (for example, should it be a linear or log-linear regression model?)

Table 4.   *The main types of migration model*

	Specification	Cross-section data	Time-series data
Fixed proportions models			
Markov chain	$M_{ij} = q_{ij} P_i$	The estimated coefficients are assumed to remain constant over time	'Naive' models that nevertheless may perform well as forecasting devices
Alternative	$M_{ij} = q'_{ij} P_i P_j$		
Regression models			
Ad hoc (linear)	$M_{ij} = f_1(P_i, P_j, D_{ij}, X_i, X_j)$	The assumption $A_{ji} = A_{ij}$ is necessary for estimation at the M_{ij} level and may take a gravitational form. The model is highly flexible since it may be estimated at all levels of aggregation	The observed pattern of migration changes as X_i, X_j, P_i and P_j vary over time
Gravity (log-linear)	$M_{ij} = f_2(P_i, P_j, D_{ij}, X_i, X_j)$	The model may be fitted only to data on M_{ij}. The gravitational hypothesis is an essential part	

The answer to the first question depends on the purpose for which the model is to be used. In general a fixed-proportions model is appropriate for forecasting future migration,[1] on the other hand a regression model is analytical in nature and intended to isolate the factors influencing migration and the size of their effects. Of course, if the factors likely to modify the fixed proportions could be established by regression methods (particularly with time-series data), then the regression model supersedes the fixed-proportions model for forecasting purposes. But such a state of affairs is unlikely, since forecasts of independent variables are needed in addition to knowledge of the factors affecting the fixed proportions.

The answer to the second question depends on the migration data available (for Great Britain there are cross-sectional data on M_{ij}). The linear and log-linear regression models may be compared by fitting both to one set of data. The criteria for determining the best individual specification of a particular model are well known (R^2s, standard errors, correct signs of variables), but criteria for judging the relative merits of log-linear

[1] It requires data on migration and population alone.

nd linear models are not well established. The R^2s are not directly comparable, because he log-linear model is normally fitted to $\log M_{ij}$ and the linear model to M_{ij}. As chapter makes clear, the use of the criterion 'best fitting model to M_{ij}' weights the result against he log-linear model unless it is fitted to M_{ij} by a non-linear method of estimation.

There is a shortage of empirical evidence on how the models compare when estimated on the same set of data. Kelley and Weiss ask whether the Markov chain model is n adequate description of the migration process by comparing a Markov chain model with wo 'economic' models.[1] Although they come to the obvious conclusion, that their Markov model is too rigid and should be modified by taking account of economic factors, he logical arguments developed are unusual. Their approach should therefore be examined n detail.

Using five-year data for the United States for the period 1955–60, a very crude wo-region model is formed:[2]

	California	Rest of United States
California	$q_{cc} = 0{\cdot}9330$	$q_{cr} = 0{\cdot}0670$
Rest of United States	$q_{rc} = 0{\cdot}0136$	$q_{rr} = 0{\cdot}9864$

The Markov assumption in this case implies that:

(a) the level of emigration from California is a constant proportion (q_{cr}) of California's population;

(b) the level of immigration to California is a constant proportion (q_{rc}) of the population in the rest of the United States.

Strictly, this model is incompatible with the full n-region model discussed above, because t considers gross migration in and out of just one region (California). The Kelley and Weiss approach suggests that a simple two-region Markov chain model should be estimated or each region, but if there are more than two regions then there is no theoretical reason why the matrices should give compatible projections. The coefficient q_{cr} may be considered the sum of a set q_{cj} from a n-region matrix, and if the q_{cj} remain constant so does q_{cr}. But $q_{rc} = \Sigma_j q_{jc} P_j/P_r$, where P_j is the population of the jth region, and P_r is the population of the rest of the country. If the n-region matrix is a Markov matrix, and the q_{jc} remain constant, the q_{rc} are bound to change because the P_j grow at different rates. However, assuming that the two-region model does display Markov properties, the estimate of the fixed point vector is $(0{\cdot}1687, 0{\cdot}8213)$,[3] which implies that the population of California (assuming natural increase trends are neutral) will tend to 16·87 per cent of the national population (from 7·89 per cent in 1955). The expression for net migration into California may be written $N_c = q_{rc} P_r - q_{cr} P_c$, or

$$\frac{N_c}{P_c} = \frac{q_{rc} P_r}{P_c} - q_{cr} . \tag{35}$$

[1] 'Markov processes and economic analysis'.

[2] Ibid. p. 281.

[3] The fixed point vector $\boldsymbol{\alpha}$ describes the equilibrium state to which the Markov process tends if the coefficients of the transition matrix $\mathbf{Q}$ do not change over time. Given a stable transition matrix, $\boldsymbol{\alpha}\mathbf{Q} = \boldsymbol{\alpha}$.

Kelley and Weiss suggest the following wage adjustment model for migration:[1]

$$\frac{N_i}{P_i} = B\frac{W_i - W_r}{W_r},\tag{36}$$

where W_i is the wage rate for the ith region, and W_r the wage rate for the rest of the country. They then ask if it is compatible with their Markov chain model. From equations (35) and (36) the two models are compatible if

$$B\frac{W_c - W_r}{W_r} = \frac{q_{rc}\,P_r}{P_c} - q_{cr}\tag{37}$$

or

$$\frac{W_c}{W_r} = 1 - \frac{q_{cr}}{B} + \frac{q_{rc}}{B}\cdot\frac{P_r}{P_c},\tag{38}$$

that is, if W_c/W_r is a linear function of P_r/P_c over time. *A priori*, there is no reason to expect a linear relationship and therefore, in general, the two models are incompatible.[2]

Following this essentially theoretical conclusion Kelley and Weiss attempt '... to ascertain whether the Markov process yields a biased prediction of migration'. From 'several hundred pages of computer print out' they conclude that 'the Markov process will understate the adjustment'.[3] Indeed the Kelley and Weiss data and the fixed point vector imply that the right hand side of (37) is $(0{\cdot}0136 \times 0{\cdot}8213)/0{\cdot}1687 - 0{\cdot}0670$ which equals $-0{\cdot}0008$, and since the left hand side is greater than zero, their conclusion is correct; there is no need to engage in a lengthy computational exercise to confirm it.

Both models are cross-sectional. Whether the Markov or the wage adjustment model is the better predictor of the behaviour of migration into California over time is a problem that cannot be solved at this stage. Kelley and Weiss attempt to discover possible systematic changes in the Markov proportions by regressing q_{rc} and q_{cr} on P_c (as a percentage of total population) using linear and log-linear forms and two sets of cross-section data. They want to know if the slope parameter is significantly different from zero in both cases. On discovering 'a pervasive tendency for q_{rc} to rise and q_{cr} to fall as P_c rises in both the 1930s and the 1950s',[4] they conclude that over time q_{rc} will rise and q_{cr} will fall as P_c changes, so that the equilibrium percentage of population in California will rise. However their evidence shows only that, in the United States, the largest regions have tended to be the regions that gain migrants; whether large regions continue to get larger is another matter,

What conclusions may be drawn from Kelley and Weiss? First, theoretical reasoning merely shows that pairs of models are only compatible under highly unlikely conditions. Secondly, the validity of each model must be demonstrated by testing it against the data,

---

[1] From the two equations $N_i/P_N = \alpha(W_i - W_r)/W_r$ and $\alpha = BP_i/P_N$, where P_N is the national population (ibid. p. 283).

[2] Although (37) is a simple condition it is confined to an appendix (ibid. section 2, p. 296). In the main text the issue is confused by the introduction of two wages functions (log-linear functions of the proportions of the national population in the corresponding region).

[3] Ibid. pp. 286, 288 and 293.

[4] Ibid. p. 292.

out time-series data needed to project future migrations and compare the forecasting performances of different models are rarely available. Thirdly, crude models (as used by Kelley and Weiss) give crude results, and a devotee of Markov chain models would argue that rejection of the crude models used by Kelley and Weiss does not constitute rejection of the Markov approach, only of crude forms of it.

CHAPTER THREE

THE DETERMINANTS OF INTERREGIONAL MIGRATION

THE CHOICE OF EQUATIONS

In this section some regression models of interregional migration, fitted to census data for the five-year period 1961–6 and the two one-year periods 1965–6 and 1960–1, are discussed, in an attempt to determine the gravitational or economic factors that affect migration. The initial problem is to establish the 'best' form of migration model. The basic choice is between linear and log-linear models, and a linear form is selected largely on grounds of convenience. As shown above, a model of the form

$$M_{ij} = P_i P_j (A_{ij} + B_1 X_i + B_2 X_j) \tag{39}$$

implies that the net migration rate is a function of the difference between the regional and national values of an explanatory variable X, so that

$$\frac{N_i}{P_i} = (B_2 - B_1)(X_i - \bar{X})\bar{P}. \tag{40}$$

The effect of variable X on net migration may immediately be deduced from an estimated M_{ij} model by forming $B_2 - B_1$.[1] In addition, it is an advantage from the estimation point of view that the linear model is fitted directly to M_{ij} and not to $\log M_{ij}$; if the log-linear version were fitted to M_{ij} a non-linear method of estimation would have to be adopted. The values of R^2 from the log-linear regressions corresponding to the regressions of table 5 are given in the last column of that table.[2] The log-linear results are similar in terms of signs and the significance of parameters, but the R^2 are slightly lower in value.

    The data used in estimation are shown in appendix A. The three dependent variables are taken from the five-year and the one-year data of the 1966 Census and the one-year data of the 1961 Census. Data on economically active migrants, the migrants most likely to respond to economic factors, are not available in sufficient detail,[3] so data for males aged 15 to 64 are used. As table 6 shows, this measure gives reasonable estimates of flows of economically active males (slightly overstated), but of course females are

---

[1] An associated t statistic indicates the significance of each variable's effect on net migration (see J. Johnston, *Econometric Methods*, New York, McGraw-Hill, 1963, p. 121–3).

[2] In table 5, R^2 for the log-linear model measures the fit of the predicted values of M_{ij} to the actual values of M_{ij}, using as predicted value the unbiased estimates of the median value of M_{ij} derived in A.G. Goldberger, 'The interpretation and estimation of Cobb–Douglas functions', *Econometrica*, vol. 36, July–October 1968, eqn. 4.18, p. 470. The quantity maximised by the estimation procedure measures the fit of the predicted values to the actual values of $\log (M_{ij}/P_i P_j)$.

[3] Economically active immigrants and emigrants for each region in 1966 are given in General Register Office, *Sample Census 1966. England and Wales. Migration Summary Tables*, table 6, but not flows between regions.

Table 5. *Linear regression results for migration-flows,[a] 1961–6*

Regression no.	Contiguity dummy (K_{ij})	Unemployment rates (U_i)	(U_j)	Employment growth (E_i)	(E_j)	Income per capita[b] (Y_i)	(Y_j)	R^2 Linear model	Log-linear model
1.[c]	1·578 (8·14)	0·169 (2·24)	−0·383 (−5·07)					0·883	0·690
2.	1·604 (7·79)			−0·079 (−4·20)	0·102 (5·42)			0·865	0·760
3.	1·650 (7·95)					−0·0022 (−2·92)	0·0048 (6·39)	0·862	0·809
4.	1·672 (8·01)					−0·0013 (−2·48)	0·0036 (6·66)	0·860	0·804
5.	1·705 (8·05)					−0·0017 (−1·47)	0·0079 (6·75)	0·856	0·757
6.	1·525 (7·35)	0·254 (1·98)	−0·465 (−3·62)	0·074 (1·52)	−0·019 (−0·38)	−0·0020 (−0·86)	−0·0012 (−0·49)	0·886	0·798
7.	1·472 (6·90)	0·237 (1·83)	−0·487 (−3·74)	0·076 (1·62)	−0·012 (−0·25)	−0·0020 (−1·16)	−0·0016 (−0·93)	0·887	0·805
8.	1·546 (7·00)	0·278 (2·17)	−0·453 (−3·54)	0·058 (1·32)	−0·023 (−0·53)	−0·0013 (−0·36)	−0·0010 (−0·29)	0·885	0·739
9.	1·641 (8·40)	0·232 (2·35)	−0·334 (−3·38)			0·0015 (1·22)	0·0013 (1·03)	0·881	0·779
10.	1·666 (8·50)	0·245 (2·50)	−0·325 (−3·31)			0·0013 (1·48)	0·0011 (1·22)	0·880	0·789
11.	1·701 (8·74)	0·233 (0·260)	−0·330 (−3·69)			0·0035 (2·12)	0·0032 (1·93)	0·881	0·722
12.	1·601 (7·43)			−0·043 (−1·09)	0·068 (1·74)	−0·0018 (−0·77)	0·0015 (0·67)	0·867	0·791
13.	1·583 (7·22)			−0·042 (−1·15)	0·073 (2·01)	−0·0015 (−0·94)	0·0007 (0·46)	0·867	0·799
14.	1·616 (7·06)			−0·059 (−1·94)	0·079 (2·62)	−0·0014 (−0·41)	0·0022 (0·62)	0·867	0·719
15.	1·584 (8·21)	0·289 (2·41)	−0·448 (−3·74)	0·053 (1·29)	−0·027 (−0·65)			0·885	0·735

[a] Based on 86 observations, t statistics shown in brackets.

[b] In regressions numbers 3, 6, 9 and 12 from Board of Inland Revenue (schedule E income per tax case), in numbers 4, 7, 10 and 13 from Department of Health and Social Security (average gross earnings of men aged 18 to 64) and in numbers 5, 8, 11 and 14 from *Family Expenditure Survey* (average household income adjusted for regional differences in working persons per household).

[c] Only regression 1 includes a constant term (see text).

omitted. Married women no doubt tend to move with their husbands. Single, widowed and divorced women aged 15 to 64 are likely to be economically active and a separate estimation for them would be interesting, but insufficient data are available.[1]

Population estimates for the final years (1966 and 1961) are adjusted for immigrants from abroad and net internal migrants in order to give appropriate measures of regional populations for each set of migration data. The gravitational factor is measured by road distance between major towns. In addition a contiguity dummy, which takes the

[1] Ibid. table 5 gives data on males and females by marital condition for counties and local authorities alone. The distinction in this table is between single women on the one hand, and married, widowed and divorced on the other.

Table 6.   *Estimates of immigrants, emigrants and net migrants*

Thousands

	Immigrants		Emigrants		Net migrants	
	Males 15–64	Economically active males	Males 15–64	Economically active males	Males 15–64	Economically active males
Five-year data, 1961–6						
North	41·36	37·79	60·95	57·03	−19·59	−19·24
Yorks. and Humberside	69·74	63·72	75·30	69·93	−5·56	−6·21
North West	78·61	72·61	81·25	74·45	−2·64	−1·84
East Midlands	75·06	70·37	57·29	52·99	+17·77	+17·38
West Midlands	75·37	71·00	77·94	71·48	−2·57	−0·48
East Anglia	46·84	43·45	33·64	31·01	+13·20	+12·44
South East	203·25	188·24	194·50	177·94	+8·75	+10·30
South West	99·73	90·25	71·90	66·71	+27·83	+23·54
Wales	38·25	35·14	41·27	38·03	−3·02	−2·89
Scotland	31·52	n.a.	65·69	n.a.	−34·17	−33·00
One-year data, 1965–6						
North	15·94	14·55	16·41	15·11	−0·47	−0·56
Yorks. and Humberside	23·73	20·45	23·04	20·90	+0·69	−0·45
North West	25·39	22·80	25·92	22·83	−0·53	−0·03
East Midlands	23·98	21·98	19·58	17·84	+4·40	+4·14
West Midlands	24·48	22·54	25·04	22·51	−0·56	+0·03
East Anglia	15·64	14·20	12·26	11·19	+3·38	+3·01
South East	62·65	57·49	67·88	60·97	−5·23	−3·48
South West	29·50	26·25	24·18	21·80	+5·32	+4·45
Wales	12·42	11·20	12·76	11·53	−0·34	−0·33
Scotland	12·92	n.a.	19·58	n.a.	−6·66	−6·78

SOURCES: *Sample Census 1966. England and Wales. Migration Summary Tables*, Pt 1, tables 3 and 6; *Scotland. Migration Tables*, Pt I, tables 3 and 6. (Migration table 6 is not published for Scotland as a whole, although it is published for Scottish subregions and conurbations, large and small burghs. Net migration into Scotland may be derived by using the identity $\Sigma_i N_i = 0$.)

value one when two regions are contiguous[1] and zero otherwise, is used to eliminate the effect on the model of any short distance migration that happens to cross regional boundaries.

Five economic variables are used in this study; two labour-market variables – the unemployment rate and employment growth – and three income variables derived from various sources.[2] Data on only one income variable (schedule E income per tax case) are available for 1960–1. Both sets of migration data from the 1966 Census were regressed on one set of data for explanatory variables. The two labour-market variables may be interpreted initially as measuring the state of demand for labour in different regions (it

[1] Except for two regional pairs – the South East and the West Midlands, and the North West and the East Midlands, where the common boundary is relatively short and does not pass through densely populated areas. A similar variable is used by Jack in 'Interregional migration in Great Britain'.

[2] Schedule E income per tax case (Board of Inland Revenue), average gross earnings of men aged 18 to 64 (Department of Health and Social Security) and average household income adjusted for regional differences in the number of working persons per household (*Family Expenditure Survey*).

possible of course to use other measures, such as the vacancy–unemployment ratio).
The other economic variable included in the analysis is income *per capita* (measured in three ways), on the grounds that migrants may respond to differences between regions in expected and actual earnings. It is possible to introduce more unusual variables, such as the new building–employment ratio used by Hart,[1] but the causal link between such variables and interregional migration is less clear.

If we use the form of relation described by (39), it remains to find an appropriate specification for A_{ij}, the component of migration that is specific to this particular pair of regions and is not explained by the regional values of the explanatory variable X. Four versions tested using the five-year data, with K the dummy variable indicating contiguity and D the distance between the regions, were:

a) $\quad A_{ij} = A_0 + A_1 D_{ij} + A_2 K_{ij}$,

b) $\quad A_{ij} = A_0 + A_1 D_{ij}$,

c) $\quad A_{ij} = A_0 + A_2 K_{ij}$,

d) $\quad A_{ij} = A_2 K_{ij}$.

Table 7. *Regression results[a] for alternative specifications of* A_{ij}[b]

	Constant	Distance between regions (D_{ij})	Contiguity dummy (K_{ij})	R^2
a)	−13·34 (− 2·55)	−0·001 (−0·61)	3·232 (9·62)	0·813
b)	−11·03 (− 1·46)	−0·010 (−3·00)		0·605
c)	−11·49 (− 2·70)		3·305 (10·57)	0·812
d)			3·025 (9·90)	0·796

[a] Based on 90 observations; unemployment rates and income *per capita* from the *Family Expenditure Survey* are explanatory variables; t statistics given in brackets.

[b] The component of migration in eqn. (39) which is not explained by regional values of the explanatory variables.

Because there are five explanatory variables, 15 regressions were estimated for each specification (all possible combinations of economic variables). One of the regressions is reported in table 7 to indicate how each specification performs. The first three all suffer from various problems. The distance parameter A_1 is expected to have a negative sign because migration is supposed to decline as distance increases, but the constant term is negative in all three cases, and the distance variable is insignificant when included together with the contiguity dummy. The fourth specification, which includes contiguity alone,[2] is more successful, particularly when the flows between the South East and East

[1] R.A. Hart, 'A model of interregional migration in England and Wales', *Regional Studies*, vol. 4, no. 3, October 1970, pp. 279–96.

[2] The constant term is omitted; the significance of this assumption is analysed in appendix B.

Anglia, and the South East and the South West are excluded from the regression as in table 5,[1] but it seemed possible that this specification was inadequate in that migration between non-contiguous regions is affected by distance. A fifth specification was therefore tried:

$$A_{ij} = A_2 K_{ij} + A_3 K'_{ij} + A_4 D'_{ij}, \tag{41}$$

where $K'_{ij} = 0$ when $K_{ij} = 1$ and vice versa, and $D'_{ij} = D_{ij}$ when $K_{ij} = 0$ and 0 when $K_{ij} = 1$ This takes into account the distances between non-contiguous regions, but when it is estimated, only one regression has a t statistic associated with A_4 greater than 1·96 (the 5 per cent level of significance, using a one-tailed test).[2] The regression is

$$\frac{M_{ij}}{P_i P_j} = \underset{(5\cdot40)}{1\cdot348 K_{ij}} + \underset{(2\cdot21)}{0\cdot010 K'_{ij}} - \underset{(-1\cdot99)}{0\cdot00002 D'_{ij}} + \underset{(3\cdot22)}{0\cdot344 U_i} -$$

$$\underset{(-2\cdot04)}{0\cdot218 U_j} + \underset{(2\cdot68)}{0\cdot0046 Y_i} + \underset{(2\cdot49)}{0\cdot0043 Y_j} \quad (\text{R}^2 = 0\cdot888),$$

where U is the unemployment rate and Y is income *per capita*.[3] The evidence clearly suggests that the specification with contiguity alone is the best, with a modification for distance between non-contiguous regions appropriate in certain cases.

This result is important because the distance variable is included almost without exception in studies of gross migration flows. The argument in favour of including a distance variable in the regression may take several forms; two candidates are that the distance variable reflects the financial or other costs of movement to the migrant, or that it reflects the cost of information or search to the migrant seeking work in alternative locations. It is not possible to distinguish the two hypotheses empirically unless direct estimates of the costs involved can be made. But the evidence suggests that once the initial 'threshold' has been overcome, and the decision taken to move outside the local labour market and the immediate environment of friends and relatives, *ceteris paribus*, a migrant is indifferent between distances of 100 and 400 miles.[4] The contiguity dummy picks up the short-distance movements that happen to cross regional boundaries, and that, in many cases, do not entail a change of workplace.

THE FIVE-YEAR RESULTS

The results from the five-year data can now be analysed in detail. The regression results are given in table 5 and the estimates and t statistics for $B_2 - B_1$ in table 8. The regression

---

[1] These flows are extremely large, and 'perverse' in the sense that the two net flows are away from the South East. This suggests that the process of migration between these three regions should be treated as a separate phenomenon (see chapter 4 below).

[2] This used 86 observations; if 90 observations are used, several regressions have incorrect signs for both A_3 and A_4.

[3] From the *Family Expenditure Survey*.

[4] This result does not exclude the distance variable being important when the migration is of short distance, see chapter 4 below.

Table 8.   *Estimates of* $B_2 - B_1$, *1961–6*

Regression number[a]	Unemployment rates	Employment growth	Income per capita
1.	−0·552		
	(−6·14)		
2.		0·181	
		(4·81)	
3.			0·0070
			(4·66)
4.			0·0049
			(4·58)
5.			0·0096
			(4·13)
6.	−0·719	−0·093	0·0008
	(−3·27)	(−1·02)	(0·33)
7.	−0·724	−0·088	0·0004
	(−3·28)	(−0·99)	(0·22)
8.	−0·731	−0·081	0·0003
	(−3·27)	(−0·96)	(0·07)
9.	−0·566		−0·0002
	(−3·49)		(−0·09)
10.	−0·570		−0·0002
	(−3·54)		(−0·13)
11.	−0·563		−0·0003
	(−5·13)		(−0·10)
12.		0·111	0·0033
		(1·55)	(1·18)
13.		0·115	0·0022
		(1·70)	(1·19)
14.		0·138	0·0036
		(2·47)	(1·10)
15.	−0·737	−0·080	
	(−3·51)	(−0·97)	

[a] See table 5.

are fitted to 86 observations and only the first has a constant term.[1] It is often assumed that, because net migration is expected to vary inversely with the unemployment rate (its $B_2 - B_1$ is negative), migrants are 'pushed' from high-unemployment regions (positive B_1) and 'pulled' to low-unemployment regions (negative B_2). But 'push'–'pull' is not the only logical possibility. A variable may have two positive or two negative signs for B_1 and B_2 with still a correct sign for the net migration parameter. In certain cases a variable may simply affect the level of gross migration, without affecting net migration at all.

When M_{ij} is regressed on each explanatory variable individually (regressions 1–5 of table 5), all variables have the appropriate 'push'–'pull' signs and all have significant effects on net migration with correct signs. What happens when groups of variables are included together in the regressions? In regressions 6, 7 and 8, which contain both labour-market variables and one of the income variables, only the unemployment rate is statistically significant. From the evidence of regression 15, the reason for the failure of these regressions is that employment growth and the unemployment rate are collinear. The unemployment rate may be judged the best labour-market variable on the grounds that,

[1] The estimate of the constant is 2·808 with t statistic 10·54. The critical value of U_i (see appendix B) is 13·14.

in table 5, the two-variable regressions 9, 10 and 11 have higher R^2s than the two-variable regressions 12, 13 and 14, while in regression 15 the unemployment rate has a $B_2 - B_1$ significantly different from zero. In regressions 9, 10 and 11, $B_2 - B_1$ for the unemployment rate is significantly negative, but for the income variable it is insignificantly negative. Net migration seems, therefore, to be determined by the unemployment rate rather than by income *per capita*.

Has income *per capita* an effect on migration? Only in regression 11 of table 5 is it significantly positive for the region of origin, although all the income parameters are positive in regressions 9, 10 and 11. The evidence suggests that high income *per capita* in a region tends to increase the level of migration from it, but regression 1 indicates that a model with a constant term and the unemployment rate as the sole independent variable generates a slightly higher R^2. It is true that the regression quoted earlier in the text (page 72) with a modified distance variable D'_{ij} has significantly positive parameters for income *per capita* in regions of origin and destination. To some extent, however, this is unsatisfactory. Inspection of the residuals (table 9) shows that movement to and from Scotland is overestimated and movement to and from the South West underestimated; the variable for physical distance is probably incapable of coping with the flows to and from these two regions. In addition the contiguity dummy is not perfect; the level of migration between the North West and the West Midlands, two contiguous regions, is considerably lower than predicted, but between the North and Yorkshire and Humberside, and between Yorkshire and Humberside and the East Midlands, the level of migration is higher than expected, probably because both York and Sheffield are close to the relevant boundaries.

The results suggest that the main factor determining net migration rates is the difference in the availability of job-opportunities between regions as reflected in observed unemployment rates. The evidence that migration is higher, *ceteris paribus*, between regions with higher income *per capita* poses considerable problems of interpretation. There are three main possibilities. First, migrants between regions of high income *per capita* may be better placed to afford the financial costs of movement (which are not inconsiderable, particularly in the case of owner—occupiers). This hypothesis would predict a significantly positive parameter for income *per capita* in the region of origin (as in regression 11 of table 5) only if the attractions of higher pay elsewhere have a relatively insignificant effect on interregional movement, and this deprives us of the most obvious explanation of significant positive coefficients in the region of destination. The second (and simplest) possibility is that the variable for income *per capita* may be picking up regional differences in the occupational composition of migrants, assuming that persons in certain occupations for which there is a national rather than a local labour market (for example, the professions) have a higher propensity to migrate. There is also a third possibility, that high labour turnover (and hence a large amount of movement including interregional movement) may be associated with high income, and that the unemployment variable fails to pick up all of this effect because (as can be demonstrated) unemployment and rate of turnover show only an imperfect negative correlation.

It is particularly important to note the relative ineffectiveness of the variable for employment growth in the regional models, since at the county level it is employment growth rather than the unemployment rate that is significantly correlated with net migration.[1]

[1] Hart, 'A model of inter-regional migration in England and Wales'.

Table 9. Residuals[a] from regression on page 72[b]

	North	Yorks. and Humberside	North West	East Midlands	West Midlands	East Anglia	South East	South West	Wales	*Thousands* Scotland	Row total[c]
North		5.8	-2.2	2.6	2.0	0.3	1.5	0.3	-0.4	-2.3	7.6
Yorks. and Humberside	5.2		0.3	8.6	-0.7	1.4	0.2	1.6	-0.3	-0.5	15.7
North West	-1.6	-2.2		0.2	-4.7	0.1	-1.4	1.9	1.0	-1.9	-8.5
East Midlands	0.5	4.8	0.2		1.5	2.7	-3.6	2.4	-0.0	-0.0	8.5
West Midlands	0.2	-1.2	-2.0	3.2		0.6	0.8	5.8	1.8	-0.3	9.1
East Anglia	0.6	0.9	-0.2	1.9	0.5			2.0	0.3	-0.0	6.1
South East	1.3	-3.3	1.5	-1.1	-1.6				2.1	-0.6	-1.6
South West	0.9	0.1	0.1	1.7	0.9	1.8			1.3	-0.4	6.4
Wales	-0.6	-1.4	-1.0	-0.4	1.2	-0.1	1.1	2.8		-1.3	0.3
Scotland	-1.5	-0.4	-0.3	2.0	-0.5	-0.2	0.2	-0.9	-1.4		-2.9
Column total[d]	4.9	3.3	-3.6	18.8	-1.2	6.6	-1.2	16.0	4.4	-7.3	
Column total *minus* row total[e]	-2.7	-12.4	5.0	10.2	-10.3	0.4	0.4	9.6	4.1	-4.4	
True N_i	-19.6	-5.6	-2.6	17.8	-2.6	2.4	33.8	13.6	-3.0	-34.1	

[a] The differences between actual values of M_{ij} and the values predicted by the regression. A negative sign indicates that the predicted value is higher than the actual value.

[b] Based on 86 observations, excluding some for East Anglia, the South East and the South West.

[c] Residuals for total emigrants.

[d] Residuals for total immigrants.

[e] Residuals for net migrants.

Results for the two sets of one-year data are given for 1965–6 in tables 10 and 11 and for 1960–1 in tables 12, 13, 14, and 15.[1] The modified specification (with distance between non-contiguous regions) is unsuccessful in both cases.

The 1965–6 regressions are broadly similar to the regressions estimated on five-year data for 1961–6, as might be expected. Only the unemployment rate has a significant effect on net migration when one explanatory variable is included and employment growth has no significant effect at all. When income *per capita* is included with the unemployment

Table 10. *Linear regression results for migration-flows,*[a] *1965–6*

	Contiguity dummy (K_{ij})	Unemployment rates (U_i)	(U_j)	Employment growth (E_i)	(E_j)	Income *per capita*[b] (Y_i)	(Y_j)	R^2
1.[c]	0·501 (8·39)	0·024 (1·02)	−0·049 (−2·09)					0·882
2.	0·503 (8·42)			−0·007 (−1·29)	0·014 (2·60)			0·879
3.	0·518 (8·53)					0·0001 (0·26)	0·0008 (3·44)	0·875
4.	0·525 (8·59)					0·0001 (0·77)	0·0006 (3·69)	0·873
5.	0·534 (8·80)					0·0006 (1·65)	0·0014 (4·12)	0·874
6.	0·479 (7·54)	0·055 (1·38)	−0·085 (−2·14)	0·018 (1·19)	0·001 (0·05)	−0·0004 (−0·49)	−0·0009 (−1·17)	0·887
7.	0·463 (7·09)	0·052 (1·30)	−0·094 (−2·34)	0·019 (1·30)	0·002 (0·16)	−0·0004 (−0·75)	−0·0009 (−1·64)	0·888
8.	0·493 (7·29)	0·067 (1·69)	−0·081 (−2·05)	0·015 (1·08)	−0·005 (−0·37)	0·0002 (0·16)	−0·0007 (−0·67)	0·886
9.	0·518 (8·58)	0·059 (1·92)	−0·052 (−1·72)			0·0008 (1·95)	0·0001 (0·14)	0·882
10.	0·526 (8·78)	0·065 (2·14)	−0·052 (−1·73)			0·0006 (2·32)	0·0001 (0·19)	0·881
11.	0·535 (9·02)	0·057 (2·05)	−0·050 (−1·81)			0·0015 (2·90)	0·0004 (0·88)	0·883
12.	0·490 (7·81)			−0·004 (−0·34)	0·018 (1·60)	−0·0004 (−0·57)	−0·0004 (−0·61)	0·880
13.	0·482 (7·55)			−0·004 (−0·42)	0·020 (1·87)	−0·0003 (−0·73)	−0·0004 (−0·94)	0·881
14.	0·499 (7·46)			−0·008 (−0·88)	0·016 (1·84)	−0·0001 (−0·05)	−0·0003 (−0·25)	0·879
15.	0·502 (8·46)	0·059 (1·58)	−0·069 (−1·87)	0·016 (1·22)	−0·008 (−0·64)			0·885

[a] Based on 86 observations; t statistics shown in brackets.

[b] In regressions numbers 3, 6, 9 and 12 from Board of Inland Revenue, in numbers 4, 7, 10 and 13 from Department of Health and Social Security, in numbers 5, 8, 11 and 14 from *Family Expenditure Survey*.

[c] Only regression 1 includes a constant term; its value is 0·794, t statistic 9·60. The critical value of U_i (assuming $U_i = U_j$) is 10·79 (see appendix B).

[1] Eight observations are missing from the 1960–1 data on the flows from the English standard regions to Scotland. The grouped observation on persons moving from England to Scotland is not used to help estimate the model, although it would be possible to do so.

ⱥgression .umber[a]	Unemployment rates	Employment growth	Income *per capita*
1.	−0·073 (−1·80)		
2.		0·021 (1·94)	
3.			0·0007 (1·59)
4.			0·0005 (1·47)
5.			0·0008 (1·24)
6.	−0·140 (−2·05)	−0·017 (−0·61)	−0·0005 (−0·60)
7.	−0·146 (−2·14)	−0·017 (−0·60)	−0·0005 (−0·83)
8.	−0·148 (−2·14)	−0·020 (−0·76)	−0·0009 (−0·89)
9.	−0·111 (−2·22)		−0·0007 (−0·91)
10.	−0·117 (−2·36)		−0·0005 (−1·08)
11.	−0·107 (−2·50)		−0·0011 (−1·03)
12.		0·022 (1·06)	−0·0000 (−0·04)
13.		0·024 (1·23)	−0·0001 (−0·17)
14.		0·024 (1·48)	−0·0002 (−0·22)
15.	−0·128 (−1·97)	−0·024 (−0·93)	

See table 10.

ⱥte (equations 9, 10 and 11) income *per capita* for the region of origin is nearly always ⱥignificantly positive.[1] Table 16 gives the residuals for regression 11 of table 10.

The results for 1960–1 differ slightly from the results for the other two sets of ⱥata. The main difference is that, with 82 observations (including the four flows be-ⱥween the South East and the South West or East Anglia), where there is a constant term ⱥt has an estimated value insignificantly different from zero in all cases (including the ⱥegression with the unemployment rate alone). The constant term is therefore omitted as ⱥefore (table 12). But when 78 observations are used, the constant term is significantly ⱥositive except where the unemployment rate is included alone (regression 1B of table 14). ⱥhe constant term is therefore retained in this table. When the explanatory variables are ⱥncluded in the equation singly (regressions 1–3 of tables 12 and 14) only employment ⱥrowth (82 observations) and income *per capita* (78 observations) have a significant effect ⱥn net migration. But the equations with several explanatory variables give more familiar ⱥesults. In regression 5 of tables 12 and 14 (corresponding to regression 9 of table 10) ⱥncome *per capita* for the region of origin has a significantly positive parameter. In terms

ⱥ Only in equation 9 of table 10 does the *t* statistic fall below a value of 2.

Table 12. *Linear regression results[a] for migration-flows, 1960–1 (82 observations)*

	Contiguity dummy (K_{ij})	Unemployment rates (U_i)	(U_j)	Employment growth (E_i)	(E_j)	Income *per capita*[b] (Y_i)	(Y_j)	R^2
1.	1·074 (9·26)	0·208 (5·12)	0·172 (3·43)					0·72
2.	0·992 (10·08)			−0·015 (−1·65)	0·022 (2·49)			0·80
3.	1·010 (9·93)					0·0001 (0·23)	0·0010 (1·63)	0·79
4.	0·909 (8·43)	0·037 (0·46)	−0·265 (−2·35)	0·016 (0·84)	0·037 (1·88)	−0·0014 (−0·78)	−0·0052 (−3·37)	0·83
5.	1·074 (10·88)	0·143 (2·27)	−0·280 (−2·97)			0·0030 (2·77)	−0·0015 (−1·43)	0·81
6.	0·896 (8·53)			−0·008 (−0·50)	0·051 (3·48)	−0·0016 (−1·06)	−0·0040 (−2·67)	0·82
7.	1·009 (10·13)	0·024 (0·34)	−0·164 (−1·51)	0·003 (0·16)	0·007 (0·38)			0·81

[a] t statistics shown in brackets.

[b] Income data from Board of Inland Revenue.

Table 13. *Estimates of $B_2 - B_1$, 1960–1 (regressions based on 82 observations)*

Regression number[a]	Unemployment rates	Employment growth	Income *per capi.*
1.	−0·036 (−0·42)		
2.		0·037 (2·07)	
3.			0·000 (0·70)
4.	−0·302 (−1·76)	0·021 (0·61)	−0·003 (−1·89)
5.	−0·423 (−3·21)		−0·004 (−2·13)
6.		0·059 (2·25)	−0·002 (−1·36)
7.	−0·188 (−1·21)	0·004 (0·11)	

[a] See table 12.

of $B_2 - B_1$ (tables 13 and 15), the unemployment rate has a significantly negative effect on net migration and so has income *per capita* when 82 observations are used (table 13). In regression 6 employment growth has a significantly positive effect and from regression 7 it is difficult to decide which labour-market variable is the better measure of job-opportunities, since multicollinearity renders the effect of both variables insignificant (except the parameter for unemployment in the region of destination in regression 7 of table 14). The residuals from regression 5 of table 14 are given in table 17.

Linear regression results[a] for migration-flows, 1960–1 (78 observations)

	Constant	Contiguity dummy (K_{ij})	Unemployment rates		Employment growth		Income per capita[b]		R²
			(U_i)	(U_j)	(E_i)	(E_j)	(Y_i)	(Y_j)	
A.		0·508	0·215	0·168					0·737
		(5·10)	(7·58)	(4·80)					
B.	26·73	0·450	0·205	0·150					0·745
	(1·52)	(4·24)	(7·11)	(4·07)					
.	33·59	0·388			−0·018	0·024			0·881
	(2·96)	(5·37)			(−3·59)	(5·00)			
.	38·48	0·376					−0·0007	0·0018	0·869
	(3·26)	(4·96)					(−1·76)	(4·49)	
.	47·78	0·422	0·059	−0·181	−0·013	0·007	0·0021	0·0001	0·896
	(3·68)	(5·84)	(1·31)	(−2·77)	(−1·08)	(0·60)	(1·79)	(0·12)	
.	45·98	0·424	0·074	−0·217			0·0014	−0·0000	0·894
	(3·92)	(5·93)	(2·00)	(−4·06)			(2·08)	(−0·02)	
.	41·08	0·393			−0·029	0·023	0·0014	0·0006	0·884
	(3·13)	(5·42)			(−2·82)	(2·31)	(1·36)	(0·57)	
.	42·27	0·397	0·019	−0·152	−0·002	0·011			0·891
	(3·58)	(5·57)	(0·48)	(−2·43)	(−0·18)	(1·08)			

[a] *t* statistics shown in brackets.

[b] Income data from Board of Inland Revenue.

Table 15. *Estimates of $B_2 - B_1$, 1960–1 (regressions based on 78 observations)*

Regression number[a]	Unemployment rates	Employment growth	Income per capita
1A.	−0·047		
	(−0·77)		
1B.	−0·055		
	(−0·92)		
2.		0·042	
		(0·50)	
3.			0·0025
			(3·12)
4.	−0·240	0·020	−0·0020
	(−2·48)	(0·95)	(−1·36)
5.	−0·291		−0·0014
	(−3·87)		(−1·07)
6.		0·052	−0·0008
		(3·03)	(−0·59)
7.	−0·171	0·013	
	(−1·94)	(0·63)	

[a] See table 14.

Table 16. *Residuals from regression 11 of table 10*

	North	Yorks. and Humberside	North West	East Midlands	West Midlands	East Anglia	South East	South West	Wales	Scotland	Row total (*Tens*)
North		169	-90	42	32	2	-32	-11	-16	-61	35
Yorks. and Humberside	172		12	245	-13	25	-44	14	-4	-22	385
North West	-29	-4		62	-148	-4	-81	36	49	-59	-178
East Midlands	29	219	52		85	64	-143	55	-3	-2	356
West Midlands	15	10	-59	141		23	88	146	24	-41	347
East Anglia	21	41	13	90	23			45	-3	-1	229
South East	73	-109	-61	-60	61				61	10	-25
South West	26	12	-1	41	34	58			32	-35	167
Wales	-20	-36	-53	–	41	9	50	41		-33	-1
Scotland	-22	-14	-3	34	-13	-11	75	-47	-55		-28
Column total	265	288	-190	595	102	166	-87	279	85	-244	
Column total *minus* row total	230	-97	-12	239	-245	-63	-62	112	86	-188	

Note: see footnotes to table 9.

Table 17. *Residuals from regression 5 of table 14*

	North	Yorks. and Humberside	North West	East Midlands	West Midlands	East Anglia	South East	South West	Wales	Scotland	*Tens* Row total
North		88	-27	11	-23	-25	12	26	-22		40
Yorks. and Humberside	-25		178	40	187	-45	-1	-10	-39		285
North West	20	-30		-46	-51	-2	-13	-132	-50		-304
East Midlands	-16	69	22		-26	110	-47	14	34		160
West Midlands	42	-84	37	-1		-50	46	-50	-93		-153
East Anglia	50	-19	41	116	61			-28	-18		203
South East	-40	114	51	-59	-65	-27			-58		-57
South West	-69	42	-21	9	-41	-33	-30		-128		-235
Wales	-1	49	40	133	-2	-13	35	-13		-6	137
Scotland	11	31	67	-65	-73		2	-65	66	-6	-6
Column total	-28	260	388	138	-33	-85	2	-258	-308	-6	
Column total *minus* row total	-68	-25	692	-22	120	-288	59	-23	-445	—	

Note: see footnotes to table 9.

81

CHAPTER FOUR

AN ANALYSIS OF COVARIANCE

In this section the covariance approach is applied to the study of interregional migration. Two models are estimated: an analysis of covariance model is fitted to data on migration between subregions of southern England, and an analysis of variance model is used to test for changes in the pattern of migration between 1960–1 and 1965–6.

SUBREGIONAL MIGRATION IN SOUTHERN ENGLAND

The application of a covariance model to data on migration is of particular value when data on explanatory variables (apart from population) are not available. The models fitted to data on interregional flows in chapter 3 do not explain the pattern of flows between the South East and East Anglia or the South West because of the large outflow of migrants from London and the increasing separation of workplace and residence. A model of migration-flows between the subregions of southern England is therefore of interest, but adequate data are not available on the explanatory variables used already and on other useful variables such as house prices. In such a situation a covariance model may be used to provide descriptive information on the pattern of migration and tests of some important hypotheses.

The covariance model used here is based on the explanatory models of the previous section. A linear model is adopted, with explanatory variables replaced by dummies for subregions of origin and destination. The model is:

$$M_{ij} = P_i P_j (A_{ij} + B_{1i} + B_{2j}),$$ (42)

where A_{ij} is a linear combination of K_{ij} = a contiguity dummy variable, D_{ij} = distance between subregions and D_{Lj} = the distance of the jth subregion from London (destination regions only);

and B_{1i} is a dummy variable for subregion of origin;

B_{2j} is a dummy variable for subregion of destination.

The dummies represent the 'push' and 'pull' factors, or differences in attractiveness between subregions. The exact specification of A_{ij} is determined in the empirical work.[1] The variable for distance from London is introduced because the matrix of migration-flows (table A.7) is dominated by out-migration from London. If a large proportion of the movement is explained by the extension of the journey to work, without change of workplace, then distance from London is of crucial importance as a factor reducing the attractiveness of distant subregions to migrants from London. From (42) the immigration rate to other subregions is

---

[1] It is convenient to omit the constant term which is not a crucial part of the model; its inclusion simply affects the interpretation of B_{1i} and B_{2j}.

$$\frac{I_i}{P_i} = \Sigma_j \frac{M_{ji}}{P_i} = \Sigma_j A_{ji} P_j + \Sigma_j B_{1j} P_j + B_{2i} \Sigma_j P_j , \tag{43}$$

and the emigration rate is:

$$\frac{E_i}{P_i} = \Sigma_j \frac{M_{ij}}{P_i} = \Sigma_j A_{ij} P_j + B_{1i} \Sigma_j P_j + \Sigma_j B_{2j} P_j . \tag{44}$$

If the condition $A_{ij} = A_{ji}$ holds (as in chapter 3), then the value of the net migration rate would be:

$$\frac{N_i}{P_i} = (B_{2i} - \bar{B}_2) \Sigma_j P_j - (B_{1i} - \bar{B}_1) \Sigma_j P_j , \tag{45}$$

where $\bar{B}_2 = \Sigma_j B_{2j} P_j / \Sigma_j P_j$ and $\bar{B}_1 = \Sigma_j B_{1j} P_j / \Sigma_j P_j$.
In this case the net migration rate is the difference of two components,[1] the 'pull' component $(B_{2i} - \bar{B}_2) \Sigma_j P_j$ and the 'push' component $(B_{1i} - \bar{B}_1) \Sigma_j P_j$. The 'pull' component summarises the attractiveness of a subregion as a destination relative to other destinations and the 'push' component summarises the attractiveness or otherwise of the subregion of origin relative to other subregions.

If the parameter of the distance from London variable is significant, then A_{Lj} does not equal A_{jL}. In this case the value of the net migration rate is given by (45) plus an additional component, which takes the value $-A_3 \Sigma_j P_j D_{Lj}$ for London and the value $A_3 P_L D_{Li}$ for all other subregions. The presence of the additional component implies that 'push' in the case of London $(A_3 B_{Lj} + B_{1L})$ varies by subregion of destination as well as of origin, so that

$$M_{Lj} = A_1 K_{ij} + (A_3 B_{Lj} + B_{1L}) + B_{2j} . \tag{46}$$

Therefore an 'overall push' component may be formed by subtracting the additional component from $(B_{1i} - \bar{B}_1) \Sigma_j P_j$.

When estimating the model given in equation (42) one dummy variable must be omitted to avoid definitional multicollinearity; let it be the last B_2 dummy, B_{2s}. The estimated parameters from a regression excluding B_{2s} are linear combinations of theoretical parameters with expected values $E(b_{1i}) = B_{1i} + B_{2s}$ and $E(b_{2i}) = B_{2i} - B_{2s}$. But the expected values for the 'push' and 'pull' components are $E[(b_{1i} - \bar{b}_1) \Sigma_j P_j] = (B_{1i} - \bar{B}_1) \Sigma_j P_j$ and $E[(b_{2i} - \bar{b}_2) \Sigma_j P_j] = (B_{2i} - \bar{B}_2) \Sigma_j P_j$, because terms in B_{2s} cancel out. Therefore the 'push' and 'pull' components and the net migration rate may be estimated, even though individual parameters cannot be estimated directly. Immigration and emigration rates may also be estimated.

In addition several hypotheses may be tested:
(a) $B_{1i} = B_1$ for all i;
(b) $B_{2i} = B_2$ for all i;
(c) (a) and (b) jointly, and
(d) $B_{1i} = B_{2i}$ for all i.
The first three are straightforward F tests on the significance of a classification,[2] whether

---

[1] The 'pull' component is not the immigration rate and the 'push' component is not the emigration rate.

[2] See Johnston, *Econometric Methods*, p. 126.

there are significant differences in 'push', in 'pull', or in both 'push' and 'pull'. But the fourth test is more unusual. If $B_{1i} = B_{2i}$, and $A_{ij} = A_{ji}$, then $M_{ij} = M_{ji}$, for all i and all j, and therefore $N_i = 0$ for all i. This therefore tests the hypothesis of zero net migration into each region, that is whether the observed flow of migrants between regions is an equal exchange. The existence of an equal pattern (or one that is nearly equal) implies that total immigrants and total emigrants are correlated, a result that sometimes surprises researchers.[1] The heavy outflow of migrants from London excludes the possibility of an equal exchange pattern of migration between the subregions of southern England, but the equal exchange test may be applied to all subregions other than London and the Outer Metropolitan area (OMA).

In the empirical work the standard subregions of the South East, the South West and East Anglia (as well as Northamptonshire from the East Midlands) are aggregated into twelve: two central subregions (Greater London and the Outer Metropolitan area), six inner subregions (Kent; the Sussex coast; the Solent; Bedfordshire, Buckinghamshire, Berkshire, Oxfordshire and Northamptonshire (BBBO and N'ton) together; north west with south west East Anglia; and Essex with south east East Anglia), and four outer subregions (the western and southern South West; the central South West; the northern South West; and north east East Anglia). Full sources and definitions of the data are given in appendix tables A.7, A.8 and A.9. As in chapter 3 the migration-flows are of males aged 15 to 64, for the period 1961–6. For the Greater London conurbation and the Outer Metropolitan area, direct estimates of this section of the population are available, but for other subregions only total population.[2] To obtain estimates of the subregional populations of males aged 15 to 64, we reduced the subregional total populations by the regional ratio of males aged 15 to 64 to total population. Distance and contiguity variables are defined as in chapter 3, but the definition of distance from the Outer Metropolitan area is arbitrary, because that area encircles Greater London and so is the only subregion contiguous with it.

The first problem is to establish the specification of A_{ij}. Table 18 gives estimated values for the parameters of contiguity (K_{ij}), distance from London (D_{Lj}) and distance (D_{ij}), as well as R^2s from regressions including B_1 and B_2 dummy variables. All variables have correct signs and all are significant when included in the regression singly or in pairs, but when all three variables are included the distance parameter is insignificant. Again contiguity is a slightly more successful variable than the distance variable (the R^2 of regression 4 is 0·991, compared with 0·985 for regression 6). Therefore regression 4 is the model used in the rest of this section, with distance from London and contiguity the two main constituents of A_{ij}.

The results of the F tests on regression 4 are given in table 19. The 'equal exchange test allows separate B_1 and B_2 dummies for Greater London and the Outer Metropolitan area, but assumes $B_{1i} = B_{2i}$ for all other subregions. In all cases the null hypotheses are rejected at the 1 per cent level of significance. The predicted values from regression 4 are given in table 20 and may be compared with the actual values given in appendix table A.7. The net outflow of migrants from London is large, so that all other regions experien

---

[1] For example, 'A puzzling phenomenon emerges from the analysis of the Census data; there is a pronounced positive association between in- and out-migration' (J.B. Lansing and E. Mueller , *The Geographic Mobility of Labor*, Ann Arbor, University of Michigan, 1969).

[2] All males plus females.

84

Table 18. *Estimates of distance and contiguity parameters*

	Contiguity dummy (K_{ij})	Distance from London (D_{Lj})	Distance between regions (D_{ij})	R^2
.	1·172 (5·31)			0·975
.		−0·0222 (−9·54)		0·983
.			−0·0214 (−5·30)	0·975
.	1·321 (9·98)	−0·0236 (−13·96)		0·991
.	0·827 (3·58)		−0·0151 (−3·58)	0·977
.		−0·0197 (−8·86)	−0·0142 (−4·46)	0·985
.	1·234 (8·32)	−0·0228 (−12·85)	−0·0036 (−1·29)	0·991

Note: t statistics are given in brackets.

Table 19. *Results of F tests on regression 4 of table 18*

	Null hypothesis	Value of F	Degrees of freedom	Approx. F at 1% level
a)	$B_{1i} = B_1$	40·17	11 × 107	2·47
b)	$B_{2i} = B_2$	13·20	11 × 107	2·47
c)	$B_{1i} = B_1$ and $B_{2i} = B_2$	490·80	24 × 107	1·86
d)	$B_{1i} = B_{2i}{}^a$	5·83	10 × 107	2·47

a For all regions of origin except Greater London and the Outer Metropolitan area.

large positive inflows, especially the Outer Metropolitan area. The predicted net migration into Bedfordshire, Buckinghamshire, Berkshire, Oxfordshire and Northamptonshire is negative, although actual net migration is positive, partly because the level of immigration from the Outer Metropolitan area is underestimated and partly because emigration to the subregions of the South West is overestimated. In addition net migration into the Outer Metropolitan area and into the South West (southern and western) from other subregions is overestimated.

The estimated values of the 'push' and 'pull' components defined earlier are given in table 21.[1] The subregions of highest 'pull' (column 4) are the South West (southern and western), Kent, the South West (central) and the Sussex coast. East Anglia (north east) is also attractive possibly because of overspill. The least attractive subregion is Bedfordshire, Buckinghamshire, Berkshire, Oxfordshire and Northamptonshire, but the actual values suggest that the value of this component may be underestimated. The size of the component $(B_{1i} - \bar{B}_1)\Sigma_j P_j$ given in column 1 indicates the ranking of each subregion's 'push' relative to other subregions (except London). 'Overall push' in column 3,

[1] It is theoretically possible to calculate t statistics for all components given in table 21, but for computational reasons the calculations were not performed.

Table 20. *Predicted subregional migration-flows*

	East Anglia			South East						South West			Total emigration
	SE & Essex	NE	NW & SW	Greater London	OMA	Kent	Sussex coast	Solent	BBBO & N'ton	Central	S & W	N	
East Anglia													
SE & Essex		84	64	191	613	48	55	56	11	47	173	86	1,428
NE	79		53	147	173	39	45	44	8	38	143	69	838
NW & SW	82	72		119	524	40	45	41	83	38	149	67	1,260
South East													
Greater London	1,238	487	618		15,393	1,225	1,618	1,660	1,184	583	502	1,021	25,529
OMA	547	155	341	4,790		566	722	962	511	210	1,001	322	10,127
Kent	45	41	22	321	596		118	73	30	51	165	102	1,564
Sussex coast	61	56	29	415	842	127		239	36	71	235	139	2,250
Solent	75	72	23	354	1,235	97	251		200	207	350	445	3,309
BBBO & N'ton	56	53	96	253	924	72	81	261		69	262	333	2,460
South West													
Central	48	44	22	321	285	56	67	191	28		283	240	1,585
S & W	74	69	29	432	428	90	105	113	32	184		167	1,723
N	91	86	30	455	509	114	130	408	235	241	408		2,707
Total immigration	2,396	1,219	1,327	7,798	21,522	2,474	3,237	4,048	2,358	1,739	3,671	2,991	
Net migration	968	381	67	−17,731	11,395	910	987	739	−102	154	1,948	284	

Note: Abbreviations for subregions defined on p. 56.

Table 21. *Estimated components of subregional net migration rates*

	'Push' (1)	Third component (2)	Overall 'push' (1) − (2) = (3)	'Pull' (4)	Net migration rate (4) − (3) = (5)
East Anglia					
SE & Essex	−6·56	−3·27	−3·29	1·36	4·65
NE	−6·75	−6·73	−0·02	2·17	2·19
NW & SW	−7·32	−4·47	−2·85	−2·49	0·36
South East					
Greater London	11·84	7·15	4·69	−2·22	−6·91
OMA	−9·19	−1·51	−7·68	0·21	7·89
Kent	−4·02	−3·27	−0·75	4·56	5·31
Sussex coast	−4·61	−3·21	−1·40	2·53	3·93
Solent	−6·79	−4·66	−2·13	−0·40	1·73
BBBO & N'ton	−6·91	−3·69	−3·22	−3·54	−0·32
South West					
Central	−4·78	−6·89	2·11	2·87	0·76
S & W	−5·80	−11·50	5·70	11·13	5·43
N	−6·52	−7·02	0·50	1·08	0·58

takes account of the 'push' from London which varies by subregion of destination as well as by origin. The Outer Metropolitan area is easily the least 'pushful' subregion. Apart from London, most 'pushful' are the three subregions of the South West, to some extent because they are distant from London. Thus, in terms of predicted net migration rates (column 5), the areas that gain most from migration are those bordering London (the Outer Metropolitan area, Kent, the Sussex coast, south east East Anglia and Essex) and the South West (southern and western).

CHANGING INTERREGIONAL MIGRATION PATTERNS

Two sets of one-year migration data are available and were used separately in chapter 3 as dependent variables of regression models. It is interesting to know whether there were changes in the pattern of migration flows between 1960−1 and 1965−6. If we suppose the basic covariance model takes the same form as (42), then the difference in the pattern of migration between the two time periods may be described by the model:

$$\left(\frac{M_{ij}}{P_i P_j}\right)_{66} - \left(\frac{M_{ij}}{P_i P_j}\right)_{61} = \Delta A_{ij} + \Delta B_{1i} + \Delta B_{2j} \tag{47}$$

where $\Delta A_{ij} = (A_{ij})_{66} - (A_{ij})_{61}$, with ΔA_{ij} the contiguity dummy,
and $\Delta B_{1i} = (B_{1i})_{66} - (B_{1i})_{61}$

$\Delta B_{2j} = (B_{2j})_{66} - (B_{2j})_{61}$, with ΔB_{1i} and ΔB_{2j} changes in 'push' and 'pull' parameters for regions of origin and destination respectively.

If the associated error term is assumed to have zero mean and variance $S^2/(P_i P_j)_{61}^2$, the equation (47) multiplied by base year populations (1960−1) is a homoscedastic model. As before, four F tests are available to test various null hypotheses:

(a) $\Delta B_{1i} = \Delta B_1$ for all i (no changes in 'push');

87

Table 22. *Observed changes in the pattern of migration between 1960–1 and 1965–6*

	North	Yorks. & Humberside	North West	East Midlands	West Midlands	East Anglia	South East	South West	Wales	Scotland	Change in total emigration
North		517	-450	-185	71	-127	-823	-176	-83		(-1,256)
Yorks. & Humberside	-195		87	75	-115	-29	-210	-310	194		(-503)
North West	265	471		64	-199	109	-892	-553	476		(-259)
East Midlands	223	682	201		121	-187	-263	-192	-225		(360)
West Midlands	379	167	682	389		-2	-165	71	-338		(1,183)
East Anglia	128	179	152	13	-3		-297	-33	64		(203)
South East	1,428	328	859	1,298	-220	3,220		180	193		(7,286)
South West	56	166	157	30	27	-135	-1,458		-386		(-1,543)
Wales	132	-9	-367	171	-597	-96	-1,029	-368		354	-1,809
Scotland	435	130	-55	-142	-442	5	102	-370	-235		-572
Change in total immigration	2,851	1,266	1,713	-1,357	2,758	-5,035	-1,751	-340			
	(3,004)	(1,580)	(1,495)	(-2,098)	(-2,550)	(-12,423)	(162)	1,469			
	2,631										
Change in net migration	(3,672)										

Note: This table gives the values of $(M_{ij}/P_iP_j)_{66} \cdot (P_iP_j)_{61} - (M_{ij})_{66}$ in absolute numbers of migrants. Because the data on migrants from the England regions to Scotland are missing, for the English regions changes in total emigration and in net migration (shown in brackets) refer to migration within England and Wales only.

88

(b) $\Delta B_{2i} = \Delta B_2$ for all i (no changes in 'pull');

(c) both (a) and (b) (no change at all in the pattern of migration) and

(d) $\Delta B_{1i} = \Delta B_{2i}$ for all i.

The fourth test, previously the 'equal exchange' test, now tests whether the pattern of *net* migration has changed significantly. The third test implicitly tests a fixed-proportions hypothesis, that $q'_{ij} = M_{ij}/P_i P_j$ remains stable over time for all i not equal to j. Given two sets of data on migration-flows, the best method of testing the assumption of stable fixed proportions, whatever the model, is by use of an analysis of variance of this type.

Two analysis of variance models were fitted to the data given in table 22 – the differences between the migration rates, $M_{ij}/P_i P_j$, of the two periods, weighted by population for the base year $(P_i P_j)_{61}$.[1] Negative signs indicate a lower migration rate in 1966 than in 1961. The contiguity dummy was included in the regression to test for a significant ΔA_{ij}, but in both models its coefficient was insignificantly different from zero,[2] so it was decided to omit the dummy. The results of the four F tests are given in table 23 for both models. All null hypotheses are rejected at the 1 per cent level of significance; thus, the pattern of migration has changed significantly between the two periods 1960–1 and 1965–6.

Table 23.   *Results of F tests on data in table 22*

	Null hypothesis	82 observations		78 observations		Approx. F at 1% level
		F	Degrees of freedom	F	Degrees of freedom	
(a)	$\Delta B_{1i} = \Delta B_1$	2·93	9 × 63	3·41	9 × 59	2·72
(b)	$\Delta B_{2i} = \Delta B_2$	8·89	9 × 63	7·97	9 × 59	2·72
(c)	$\Delta B_{1i} = \Delta B_1$ and $\Delta B_{2i} = \Delta B_2$	7·46	18 × 63	7·85	18 × 59	2·20
(d)	$\Delta B_{1i} = \Delta B_{2i}$	10·09	9 × 63	12·28	9 × 59	2·72

The region with the largest absolute change in net migration is the South East because the increased rate of outflow to East Anglia is the main (but not the only) cause of an increase in the South East's total emigration rate and because immigration rates into the South East have fallen. The three northern regions of England (the North, Yorkshire and Humberside, and the North West) all have higher total immigration rates and lower total emigration rates, in contrast to the West Midlands and the South East. The rate of outflow from the South West to the South East has fallen, but rates of inflow from other regions to the South West have also fallen. Wales has experienced reductions in emigration rates, particularly to the South East, and immigration rates to the East Midlands have tended to increase. In both cases the South East figures prominently.

Table 24 gives the values of the changes in 'push' and 'pull' components, and in net

[1] Again the models are estimated on 82 and 78 observations. In the second case, the four observations for the South East and East Anglia, and the South East and the South West are omitted.

[2] Its t statistics were $-1·80$ and $-1·15$ for the models estimated on 82 and 78 observations respectively.

Table 24. *Estimated changes in net migration rates and their components between 1960–1 and 1965–6*

	'Push' components		'Pull' components		Net migration rates	
	82 observations	78 observations	82 observations	78 observations	82 observations	78 observations
North	−1·468 (−1·68)	−1·513 (−2·43)	1·956 (2·05)	2·535 (3·74)	3·424 (2·70)	4·048 (4·55)
Yorks. & Humberside	0·060 (0·10)	0·023 (0·05)	−0·350 (−0·47)	0·236 (0·44)	−0·410 (−0·44)	0·213 (0·32)
North West	−0·399 (−0·83)	−0·421 (−1·16)	−0·607 (−0·95)	−0·006 (−0·01)	−0·208 (−0·28)	0·415 (0·78)
East Midlands	0·473 (0·54)	0·429 (0·68)	1·239 (1·29)	1·818 (2·66)	0·766 (0·60)	1·389 (1·55)
West Midlands	0·734 (1·24)	0·699 (1·62)	−2·292 (−3·18)	−1·704 (−3·28)	−3·025 (−3·40)	−2·402 (−3·82)
East Anglia	−0·197 (−0·11)	1·462 (0·64)	11·386 (6·18)	−1·350 (−0·64)	11·582 (4·47)	−2·812 (−0·91)
South East	1·056 (2·83)	0·537 (1·92)	−1·926 (−3·53)	−1·501 (−3·85)	−2·983 (−5·59)	−2·038 (−5·07)
South West	−2·445 (−2·93)	−0·362 (−0·35)	−2·357 (−2·56)	−3·496 (−3·53)	0·088 (0·07)	−3·133 (−2·22)
Wales	−3·151 (−2·95)	−3·198 (−4·23)	−1·364 (−1·21)	−0·787 (−0·99)	1·787 (1·23)	2·411 (2·37)
Scotland	0·314 (0·56)	0·263 (0·64)	6·434 (1·59)	6·779 (2·40)	6·120 (1·50)	6·516 (2·28)

Note: t statistics are given in brackets.

migration rates predicted from the two models.[1] Predicted values of the weighted changes in migration rates from the two models are given in tables 25 and 26. Apart from East Anglia and the South West the values of change in 'push' and in 'pull' do not differ much between the two models. In the case of East Anglia the increased pull of migrants due to the inflow from the South East drops sharply in value when the South East observation is omitted, and 'push' increases in value. The regions with the largest increase in 'pull' are the North, Yorkshire and Humberside (in the second model), the East Midlands and Scotland, but in the last case the value of the component is based on one observation only, the flow from Wales to Scotland, and would be unlikely to have the same value if all observations were available. Other regions, particularly the West Midlands, have experienced relative declines in 'pull', whereas the North and Wales had the largest falls in 'push'. In terms of net migration rates the regions divide into two groups: the West Midlands, East Anglia, the South East and the South West all have reduced net in-migration rates and the North, Yorkshire and Humberside, the North West, the East Midlands, Wales and Scotland all have increased net in-migration rates.

If, as argued in chapter 3, the process of interregional migration is dependent on the general state of the national labour market, then the narrowing of net migration rates between the two years does not reflect a long-run trend, but results simply from the high level of demand for labour in the period immediately preceding the deflation of July 1966. One expects, first, that the level of turnover between industries, and presumably regions, will be higher in a period of high demand for labour, and secondly, that regional differences in net migration rates will be more marked in periods of (relatively) low demand for labour. The first point is confirmed by the evidence that turnover was 9 per cent higher in 1965—6 than in 1960—1, although the population of males aged 15 to 64 rose only by 4 per cent between the two periods.[2] The second point appears to be confirmed by the evidence presented here, although the evidence from the 1971 Census will provide an important test of both hypotheses, since the state of demand for labour in 1970—1 differs radically from that in 1965—6.

---

[1] The estimate of the changes in the net migration rate is calculated from the form given in equation (45) above, which assumes there are no missing observations, so that predictions of the missing observations are made implicitly.

[2] The turnover data exclude the four observations between the South East and East Anglia or the South West. The data on population are taken from Central Statistical Office, *Abstract of Regional Statistics*, no. 4, 1968, table 5.

Table 25. *Predicted changes in the pattern of migration between 1960–1 and 1965–6 (82 observations)*

	North	Yorks. & Humberside	North West	East Midlands	West Midlands	East Anglia	South East	South West	Wales	Scotland	Change in total emigration
North		−70	−131	53	−269	337	−765	−189	−94		(−1,128)
Yorks. & Humberside	283		92	215	−166	545	−378	−120	−19		(452)
North West	335	56		241	−322	731	−823	−230	−74		(−86)
East Midlands	224	108	117		−75	393	−130	−56	9		(590)
West Midlands	371	203	232	298		619	−70	−59	34		(1,628)
East Anglia	86	22	15	64	−67		−165	−48	−13		(−106)
South East	1,329	818	973	1,085	−91	2,088		−85	199		(6,316)
South West	38	−169	−270	−10	−384	322	−1,140		−153		(−1,766)
Wales	−7	−184	−283	−45	−355	232	−1,072	−247		354	−1,607
Scotland	333	145	151	259	−142	604	−282	−104	3		967
Change in total immigration	2,992	929	896	2,160	−1,871	5,871	−4,825	−1,138	−108		
Change in net migration	(3,787)	(332)	(831)	(1,311)	(−3,357)	(5,373)	(−10,859)	(732)	1,499		

Note: See footnote to table 22.

Table 26. *Predicted changes in the pattern of migration between 1960–1 and 1965–6 (78 observations)*

	North	Yorks. & Humberside	North West	East Midlands	West Midlands	East Anglia	South East	South West	Wales	Scotland	Change in total emigration
North		-48	-98	68	-244	-65	-738	-290	-82		(-1,497)
Yorks. & Humberside	305		141	237	-131	-25	-336	-263	-1		(-73)
North West	368	104		274	-269	-62	-755	-426	-47		(-813)
East Midlands	239	130	150		-51	-5	-103	-156	21		(225)
West Midlands	396	238	284	322		5	-24	-213	54		(1,062)
East Anglia	146	107	134	123	24			-41	36		(529)
South East	1,251	710	832	1,008	-206				135		(3,730)
South West	199	61	52	149	-137	-31			-22		(271)
Wales	5	-166	-256	-33	-335	-95	-1,051	-330		354	-1,907
Scotland	356	179	201	282	-105	-16	-244	-261	19		411
Change in total immigration	3,265	1,315	1,440	2,430	-1,454	(-294)	(-3,251)	(-1,980)	113	354	
Change in net migration	(4,406)	(1,208)	(2,052)	(1,923)	(-2,411)	(-807)	(-6,737)	(-1,990)	2,020		

Note: See footnote to table 22. Also in this table the row and column totals for East Anglia, the South East, and the South West are affected by the omission of the four observations on the changes in migration-flows between the South East and East Anglia, and the South East and South West. The changes in net migration for the three regions therefore exclude the four observations.

CHAPTER FIVE

CONCLUSIONS

In previous work on migration, particularly research using census data, the gravity model has been used to explain migration-flows — a log-linear model with distance between regions included as a major explanatory variable. In this paper a simple linear model of migration is adopted of the form:

$$M_{ij} = P_i P_j (A_2 K_{ij} + B_1 X_i + B_2 X_j),$$ (48)

where M_{ij} is migration from region i to region j,

$\quad P_i$ and P_j are populations of region i and region j,

$\quad K_{ij}$ is a contiguity dummy variable,

and $\quad X_i$ and X_j are explanatory variables for region i and region j.

This was applied to all sets of data, but for 1960–1 (78 observations) a constant term was added. The contiguity dummy is in place of a distance variable.

The main factor determining the net flows of males aged 15 to 64 between the standard regions of Great Britain is the unemployment rate. Employment growth is a less satisfactory measure of job-opportunities. Income *per capita* has no effect on net migration when included in a regression that also includes the unemployment rate, but there is evidence from all sets of data that the level of out-migration from high-income regions is higher than the level of in-migration from low-income regions. On the other hand, the linear model with a constant term,[1] $M_{ij} = P_i P_j (A_0 + A_2 K_{ij} + B_1 X_i + B_2 X_j)$, where the unemployment rate is the only economic variable, gives similar results in terms of R^2 for 1961–6 and 1965–6; thus, the evidence on the role of income *per capita* is not conclusive.

The models of interregional migration do not explain the migration-flows between the subregions of southern England, which are dominated by the outflow of migrants from London. An analysis of covariance model was estimated in chapter 4 to summarise the pattern of these migration-flows. In this model contiguity and distance from London (subregions of destination only) are both significant with correct signs, but the full distance variable is insignificant when included in regressions with the other two variables. The subregions with the highest net in-migration rates tend to be those bordering London (the Outer Metropolitan area, Kent, the Sussex coast, south east East Anglia and Essex) but the South West (southern and western) also pulls migrants.

Finally, two analysis of variance models were estimated to test for changes in the pattern of migration between 1960–1 and 1965–6. The two sets of one-year data imply migration rates that differ significantly. Apart from the large increase in the rate of migration from the South East and East Anglia, the evidence suggests that net in-migration rates to the West Midlands, East Anglia, the South East and the South West have declined

---

[1] See appendix B.

ut net migration rates to the North, Yorkshire and Humberside, the North West, the East Midlands, Wales and Scotland have increased.

APPENDIX A

DATA FOR THE MODELS

Table A.1. *Male migrants aged 15–64, five-year data, 1961–6*

	North	Yorks. & Humberside	North West	East Midlands	West Midlands	East Anglia	South East	South West	Wales	Scotland	Total emigrants (*Tens*)
North		1,329	680	584	678	159	1,765	330	172	398	6,095
Yorks. & Humberside	1,069		1,245	1,505	532	293	1,912	475	221	278	7,530
North West	575	1,152		648	969	234	2,724	702	778	343	8,125
East Midlands	224	1,105	510		853	451	1,787	460	160	179	5,729
West Midlands	276	489	1,069	1,050		231	2,479	1,236	675	289	7,794
East Anglia	131	250	165	386	232		1,690	301	102	107	3,364
South East	982	1,461	2,330	2,055	2,138	2,766		5,407	1,086	1,225	19,450
South West	262	354	436	428	772	282	3,980		448	228	7,190
Wales	109	209	628	205	729	85	1,395	662		105	4,127
Scotland	508	625	798	645	634	183	2,593	400	183		6,569
Total immigrants	4,136	6,974	7,861	7,506	7,537	4,684	20,325	9,973	3,825	3,152	
Net migration	−1,959	−556	−264	1,777	−257	1,320	875	2,783	−302	−3,417	
Immigrants from abroad	1,005	2,585	3,194	1,719	3,803	1,348	20,420	2,179	768	1,852	

SOURCES: *Sample Census 1966. England and Wales. Migration Summary Tables* and *Scotland. Migration Tables*, Pt I, table 3.

Note: The estimates are given in tens because they are based on a 10% sample of the population.

Table A.2. *Male migrants aged 15–64, one-year data, 1965–6*

	North	Yorks. & Humberside	North West	East Midlands	West Midlands	East Anglia	South East	South West	Wales	Scotland	Total emigrants
North		382	193	133	171	44	447	83	51	137	1,641
Yorks. & Humberside	349		387	446	162	78	561	131	78	112	2,304
North West	222	396		226	289	71	786	204	264	134	2,592
East Midlands	90	412	189		296	128	572	133	52	86	1,958
West Midlands	116	184	350	360		80	747	373	190	104	2,504
East Anglia	52	94	81	157	81		610	84	24	43	1,226
South East	446	524	757	701	753	987		1,680	390	550	6,788
South West	98	136	159	130	269	99	1,309		148	70	2,418
Wales	41	67	177	74	230	25	438	168		56	1,276
Scotland	180	178	246	171	197	52	795	94	45		1,958
Total immigrants	1,594	2,373	2,539	2,398	2,448	1,564	6,265	2,950	1,242	1,292	
Net migration	−47	69	−53	440	−56	338	−523	532	−34	−666	
Immigrants from abroad	433	624	982	450	853	524	5,976	809	253	2,127	

SOURCES: as table A.1.

97

Table A.3. *Male migrants aged 15–64, one-year data, 1960–1*

	North	Yorks. & Humberside	North West	East Midlands	West Midlands	East Anglia	South East	South West	Wales	Scotland	*Tens* Total emigrants
North		309	228	143	152	54	501	96	57		(1,540)
Yorks. & Humberside	349		353	404	160	75	539	153	54		(2,087)
North West	184	323		203	286	55	818	246	202		(2,317)
East Midlands	62	312	155		257	136	550	142	71		(1,685)
West Midlands	70	152	254	287		73	696	335	210		(2,077)
East Anglia	36	69	60	142	74		589	81	16		(1,067)
South East	275	451	616	512	707	583		1,534	345		(5,023)
South West	87	110	133	117	244	105	1,355		178		(2,329)
Wales	26	64	204	52	273	33	512	195		20	1,379
Scotland	135	161	247	180	234	50	761	129	68		1,965
Total immigrants	1,224	1,951	2,250	2,040	2,387	1,164	6,321	2,911	1,201	993	
Net migration	(−451)	(−297)	(−314)	(175)	(76)	(47)	(537)	(453)	(−178)	−972	
Immigrants from abroad	342	687	819	497	1,003	387	6,227	729	297	711	

SOURCES: *Census 1961. England and Wales* (special tabulations) and *Scotland.* vol. 8, *Internal Migration*, table 17.

Note: Because emigrants from England to Scotland are not classified by region, figures for the English regions for total emigrants and net migration (shown in brackets) are for migration within England and Wales only.

Table A.4. *Regional populations at the beginning of each migration period (males aged 15–64)*

	1960	1961	Tens 1965
North	102,749	106,324	104,984
Yorks. & Humberside	146,090	150,101	151,437
North West	203,405	207,970	209,971
East Midlands	101,858	103,884	106,490
West Midlands	157,321	162,784	165,533
East Anglia	48,626	48,952	50,758
South East	510,216	525,575	541,417
South West	108,008	108,288	111,909
Wales	83,731	85,554	85,801
Scotland	158,741	159,655	156,629

SOURCES: as tables A.1–A.3; *Abstract of Regional Statistics*, no. 4, 1968, table 5; *Registrar General's Quarterly Return*, no. 480, 4th quarter 1968 London, HMSO, 1969.

Note: These populations were calculated by subtracting net migrants and immigrants from abroad from the populations in 1961, 1966 and 1966 respectively.

Table A.5. *Regional distance[a] and contiguity[b]*

	North	Yorks. & Humberside	North West	East Midlands	West Midlands	East Anglia	South East	South West	Wales	Scotland
North		91	140½	153	200	256	273	327	253	143
Yorks. & Humberside	1		66½	67	109	173	190	237	166	210
North West	1	1		83½	84½	199½	190½	203	113	211½
East Midlands	0	1	0		50	124	122	180	154	276
West Midlands	0	0	1	1		156	110	130	114	287
East Anglia	0	0	0	1	0		111	248	270	378
South East	0	0	0	1	0	1		145	212	392
South West	0	0	0	0	1	0	1		165	409
Wales	0	0	1	0	1	0	0	1		312
Scotland	1	0	0	0	0	0	0	0	0	

[a] Road distance in miles between major towns in the regions from *AA Members Handbook, 1964–5*. The towns used were:

North	Newcastle-upon-Tyne
Yorks. and Humberside	Leeds
North West	Liverpool and Manchester (average distance)
East Midlands	Nottingham
West Midlands	Birmingham
East Anglia	Norwich
South East	London
South West	Taunton
Wales	Aberystwyth
Scotland	Glasgow.

[b] Pairs of regions which are contiguous were given the value 1 (except for two pairs, see p. 70 fn. 1), otherwise this dummy is 0.

Table A.6. *Explanatory variables*

	Unemployment rate[a]	Employment growth[b]	Income *per capita*[c] (1)	(2)	(3)
1961	%	%	£ p.a.	£ p.a.	s. per week
North	2·69	96·4	644·5		
Yorks. & Humberside	1·66	103·1	625·2		
North West	2·41	101·5	618·2		
East Midlands	1·26	103·6	636·9		
West Midlands	1·39	105·2	671·1		
East Anglia	2·03	106·2	567·1		
South East	1·35	106·2	690·0		
South West	2·06	105·4	590·1		
Wales	3·14	101·5	624·3		
Scotland	3·94	99·4	585·0		
1966					
North	3·86	98·4	842·4	947·0	346·2
Yorks. & Humberside	1·66	101·7	843·4	969·5	360·1
North West	2·55	99·9	864·3	995·5	342·1
East Midlands	1·38	103·2	872·1	987·0	348·0
West Midlands	1·64	105·5	922·7	1059·0	358·6
East Anglia	1·85	106·7	824·1	944·5	349·6
South East	1·39	103·9	963·4	1132·4	421·0
South West	1·90	103·3	841·6	960·0	374·0
Wales	3·03	98·7	861·4	971·5	372·5
Scotland	4·16	98·5	813·6	928·0	338·6

[a] Average rates over the periods 1957–60 and 1961–5 respectively, calculated from average numbers of unemployed from *Abstract of Regional Statistics*, no. 3, 1967, table 7.

[b] Ratios of male employees in employment 1963 : 1959 and 1966 : 1961, calculated from *Ministry of Labour Gazette*, December 1965, pp. 533–7; East Anglia Planning Board, *East Anglia – review of population and employment*, Norwich, 1966; East Anglia Economic Planning Council, *East Anglia – a study*, London, HMSO, 1968, pp. 11; unpublished estimates by the Department of Employment.

[c] (1) Average employment income (schedule E) per tax case in 1959/60, and 1964/5 averaged with 1965/6, from *106th Report of the Commissioners of Inland Revenue*, Cmnd 2283, London, HMSO, 1964, table 76; *Abstract of Regional Statistics*, no. 3, 1967, table 43 and no. 4, 1968, table 44.

(2) Average gross earnings of men aged 18–64 in civil employment 1964/5 and 1965/6 from *Abstract of Regional Statistics*, no. 3, 1967, table 45.

(3) Average household income adjusted for the average number of workers per household, 1964–6, from *Abstract of Regional Statistics*, no. 4, 1968, tables 50 and 51.

Table A.7. *Migration-flows of males aged 15–64 between subregions of southern England, 1961–66*

Tens

	East Anglia			South East						South West			Total emigration
	SE & Essex	NE	NW & SW	Greater London	OMA	Kent	Sussex coast	Solent	BBBO & N'ton	C	S & W	N	
East Anglia													
SE & Essex		166	140	302	428	37	28	65	58	28	49	68	1,369
NE	137		161	168	155	13	23	34	54	13	19	44	821
NW & SW	146	154		248	283	26	27	57	141	24	49	85	1,240
South East													
Greater London	1,087	427	584		15,563	1,197	1,457	1,534	836	419	840	868	24,812
OMA	839	289	336	4,598		684	1,069	1,156	1,084	363	607	620	11,645
Kent	30	9	18	382	538		91	86	57	37	92	51	1,343
Sussex coast	27	23	31	537	695	99		215	65	49	218	83	1,916
Solent	47	40	57	627	826	68	192		185	461	75	271	2,992
BBBO & N'ton	68	59	140	448	678	40	83	191		68		221	2,071
South West													
Central	25	9	33	264	271	25	32	446	77		244	401	1,827
S & W	37	23	40	419	341	38	67	269	82	254		360	1,930
N	51	36	81	501	477	42	77	320	241	416	303		2,545
Total immigration	2,494	1,235	1,621	8,494	20,255	2,269	3,146	4,373	2,880	2,132	2,540	3,072	
Net migration	1,125	414	381	−16,318	8,610	926	1,230	1,381	809	305	610	527	
Immigrants from 'abroad'[a]	1,078	682	1,812	19,787	8,557	734	1,132	2,655	3,189	1,100	2,471	3,239	

SOURCE: *Sample Census 1966* (special tabulations).

[a] Including those from the rest of Great Britain.

Table A.8.   *Estimated male population aged 15–64 for subregions of southern England, 1961*

	Tens
East Anglia	
South east and Essex	20,831
North east	17,373
North west and south west	18,828
South East	
Greater London	256,691
Outer Metropolitan area	144,423
Kent	17,123
Sussex coast	25,104
Solent	42,686
BBBO and Northampton	32,225
South West	
Central	20,230
Southern and western	35,847
Northern	48,917

SOURCE: General Register Office, *Registrar General's Quarterly Return for England and Wales*, no. 480, 4th quarter 1968, London, HMSO, 1969, app. E and I.

Note: For all subregions except Greater London and the Outer Metropolitan area, subregional populations of males aged 15–64 in 1966 are estimated by multiplying total subregional populations by the ratio of the regional population of males aged 15–64 to total regional population – approximately 0·3. Populations in 1961 can then be derived by subtracting net in-migration from other subregions and immigration from the rest of Great Britain and abroad (table A.7).

Table A.9. *Subregional distance [a] and contiguity [b]*

	East Anglia			South East						South West		
	SE & Essex	NE	NW & SW	Greater London	OMA	Kent	Sussex coast	Solent	BBBO & N'ton	C	S & W	N
East Anglia												
SE & Essex		60	68	54	39	86	108	131	98	168	244	169
NE	*1*		47	111	96	146	168	189	125	220	298	208
SW & NW	*1*	*1*		74	59	121	125	149	85	180	259	168
South East												
Greater London	*0*	*0*	*0*		25	54	53	77	61	114	190	116
OMA	*1*	*0*	*1*	*1*		39	38	62	45	99	175	101
Kent	*0*	*0*	*0*	*0*	*1*		63	121	115	167	242	169
Sussex coast	*0*	*0*	*0*	*0*	*1*	*1*		62	106	116	188	136
Solent	*0*	*0*	*0*	*0*	*1*	*0*	*1*		86	55	125	75
BBBO & N'ton	*0*	*0*	*1*	*0*	*1*	*0*	*0*	*1*		105	179	85
South West												
Central	*0*	*0*	*0*	*0*	*0*	*0*	*0*	*1*	*0*		81	47
S & W	*0*	*0*	*0*	*0*	*0*	*0*	*0*	*0*	*0*	*1*		96
N	*0*	*0*	*0*	*0*	*0*	*0*	*0*	*1*	*1*	*1*	*0*	

[a] Road distance in miles between major towns in the subregions from *AA Member's Handbook 1964–5*. The towns used were:

East Anglia			
SE & Essex	Colchester	Sussex coast	Brighton
NE	Norwich	Solent	Southampton
NW & SW	Cambridge and Peterborough (average distance)	BBBO & N'ton	Oxford and Northampton (average distance)
South East		South West	
Greater London	London	Central	Taunton and Salisbury (average distance)
OMA	London *minus* 15	S & W	Exeter and Plymouth (average distance)
Kent	Maidstone and Dover (average distance)	N	Bristol.

The distance from London variable, D_{Lj}, is the same as the distance variable, D_{ij}, except that $D_{Lj} = 0$ when $i \neq 1$.

[b] Pairs of subregions which are contiguous were given the value 1, otherwise this dummy is 0.

THE PROBLEM OF THE CONSTANT TERM

The model $M_{ij}/P_iP_j = A_0 + A_2K_{ij} + B_1X_i + B_2X_j$ was fitted to the 1961–6 data (86 observations), but in most regressions A_0 was insignificantly different from zero, so the constant term was omitted from the specification (because $M_{ij}/P_iP_j > 0$ for all values of X_i and X_j, and therefore A_0 should be non-negative). Dropping the constant term amount to imposing the constraint $A_0 = 0$. It is possible to argue that the model with a constant term could and should be used in migration research, even if such a model implies that M_{ij}/P_iP_j may be negative (when 90 observations are used, A_0 is significantly negative).[1]

Table B.1. *Critical values of* X_i

Variable	Parameters			Critical value
X_i	A_0	B_1	B_2	$-A_0/(B_1 + B_2)$
Employment growth	−23·953	0·0370	0·2200	93·0
Income *per capita*				
Board of Inland Revenue	−3·295	0·0012	0·0050	526·8
Department of Social Security	−3·159	0·0013	0·0040	599·5
Family Expenditure Survey	−9·789	0·0126	0·0193	306·6

There are two cases of interest, in both of which the line of argument is that a straight line is being fitted to the data when in fact the true relationship is non-linear. In the first case, if we assume that M_{ij}/P_iP_j increases with X_i (as before we assume $X_i = X_j$), and if the true curve is non-linear (curve A in chart B.1), the model with a constant term (curve B) is better than the proportional model (curve C) because it approximates to a segment of the non-linear curve. But the model with a constant term is only valid for a restricted range of values of X_i. An alternative argument is that the true model is linear, probably passing through the origin, and the reason for the negative sign of its constant term is the presence of certain observations in the sample (above the mean value of X_i) with extremely high values of M_{ij}/P_iP_j – for example, the four observations of flows between the South East and the South West or East Anglia. Therefore, omission of the extreme observations should lead to a sharp improvement in the fit of the proportional model, as is observed. In addition, in the linear model with a constant term, its value

---

[1] A critical value of X_i (assuming that $X_i = X_j$) may be calculated for the regressions including the constant term and one explanatory variable. The critical value is the lowest value of X_i at which M_{ij}/P_iP_j is non-negative, ignoring the contiguity dummy. The expression for the critical value is $-A_0/(B_1 + B_2$. If more than one variable is included in the regression, then there exists a series of joint critical values of the various explanatory variables. Table B.1 gives the critical values for the four single-variable regressions (90 observations) in which A_0 is negative. The critical values fall well below the range of variation of the sample values of each variable (table A.6).

Chart B.1.   *Linear approximation to a non-linear model* (M_{ij}/P_iP_j *increasing with* X_i)

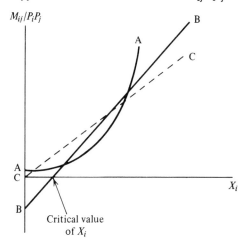

Chart B.2.   *Linear approximation to a non-linear model* (M_{ij}/P_iP_j *decreasing as* X_i *increases*)

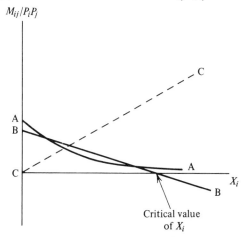

estimated on a sample of observations excluding extreme values should be insignificantly different from zero or significantly positive. This result is also observed.

When the model is fitted to 86 observations (1961–6 data), the constant term is only significantly different from zero in one regression – that including unemployment rates alone (a special case which is discussed below). In all other regressions the constant term is insignificantly different from zero, with a positive sign five times and a negative sign nine times. There is clear evidence, therefore, that the constant term should be omitted from the linear regressions fitted to the 1961–6 data.

Now consider the case where M_{ij}/P_iP_j declines as the value of the explanatory variable X_i increases. The unemployment rate is the only variable used in this paper likely to satisfy this condition. In this case the true curve slopes downwards, with a positive intercept on the M_{ij}/P_iP_j axis, and is presumably a non-linear curve asymptotic to the X_i axis (curve A of chart B.2). Then the fitted straight line requires a constant term (curve B) in order to approximate to the true curve. Using 1961–6 data, the estimated regression is regression 1 of table 5.

ECONOMIC AND SOCIAL STUDIES

*XIX *The Antitrust Laws of the U.S.A.: A Study of Competition Enforced by Law* by A.D. NEALE. 2nd edition, 1970. pp. 544. £4.00 net.

XX *A Study of United Kingdom Imports* by M. FG. SCOTT. 1963. pp. 270. £3.00 net.

*XXI *Industrial Growth and World Trade* by A. MAIZELS. 1963, reprinted with corrections 1971. pp. 563. £4.20 net.

XXIII *The British Economy in 1975* by W. BECKERMAN and ASSOCIATES. 1965. pp. 631. £4.00 net.

XXIV *Occupation and Pay in Great Britain, 1906–60* by G. ROUTH. 1965. pp. 182. £1.75 net.

XXV *Exports and Economic Growth of Developing Countries* by A. MAIZELS assisted by L.F. CAMPBELL-BOROSS and P.B.W. RAYMENT. 1968. pp.445. £3.00 net.

XXVI *Urban Development in Britain: Standards, Costs and Resources, 1964–2004* by P.A. STONE. Vol. 1: *Population Trends and Housing.* 1970. pp. 434. £3.00 ne

XXVII *The Framework of Regional Economics in the United Kingdom* by A.J. BROWN 1972. pp. 372. £4.00 net.

* Also available as a paperback in NIESR Student's Edition.

OCCASIONAL PAPERS

XXI *Pricing and Employment in the Trade Cycle: A Study of British Manufacturing Industry, 1950–61* by R.R. NEILD. 1963. pp. 73. £0.75 net.

XXII *Lancashire Textiles: A Case Study of Industrial Change* by CAROLINE MILES. 1968. pp. 124. £1.05 net.

XXIV *The Economic Impact of Commonwealth Immigration* by K. JONES and A.D. SMITH. 1970. pp. 186. £1.75 net.

XXV *The Analysis and Forecasting of the British Economy* by M.J.C. SURREY. 1971. pp. 120. £1.20 net.

XXVI *Mergers and Concentration in British Industry* by P.E. HART, M.A. UTTON and G. WALSHE. 1973. pp. 190. £1.80 net.

NIESR STUDENTS' EDITION

. *Growth and Trade* (an abridged version of *Industrial Growth and World Trade*) by A. MAIZELS. 1970. pp. 312. £1.45 net.

. *The Antitrust Laws of the U.S.A.* (2nd edition, unabridged) by A.D. NEALE. 1970. pp. 544. £1.85 net.

. *The Management of the British Economy, 1945–60* (unabridged) by J.C.R. DOW. 1970. pp. 464. £1.10 net.

REGIONAL PAPERS

. *The Anatomy of Regional Activity Rates* by JOHN BOWERS and *Regional Social Accounts for the United Kingdom* by V.H. WOODWARD. 1970. pp. 192. £1.25 net.

published by

THE CAMBRIDGE UNIVERSITY PRESS

and available through booksellers

NATIONAL INSTITUTE ECONOMIC REVIEW

published and distributed by

NIESR

2 Dean Trench St., Smith Square, London SW1P 3HE

A quarterly review of the economic situation and prospects. Annual subscription £6.00; single issues £1.75 each. Back numbers available from Wm. Dawson & Sons Ltd., Cannon House, Park Farm Rd., Folkestone, Kent (price £2.00 each plus postage).

107

Regional Unemployment Differences in Great Britain

P. C. CHESHIRE

Interregional Migration Models and their Application to Great Britain

R. WEEDEN

This volume contains two further papers of a series written by members of the team at the National Institute, led by Professor A. J. Brown, which was studying regional economic developments in the United Kingdom.

'Regional Unemployment Differences' by P. C. Cheshire sets out to examine the nature, and as far as possible the causes, of these unemployment differences. After examining the effect of labour-market imperfections, both before and after their marked increase from 1966 onwards, it concludes that they were decidedly less influential than variations in the pressure of demand between different regions.

'Interregional Migration Models' surveys the literature in this field and compares the various models, with particular reference to data available for Great Britain. It also gives the main results for the model eventually chosen to analyse migration-flows in the overall results of the project, which were published in 1972 as *The Framework of Regional Economics in the United Kingdom* by Professor Brown.

£2 NET IN U.K. $6.50 IN U.S.A.

0 521 20376 7